# MISSIONHIVE OS

AN OPERATING SYSTEM FOR MISSION-DRIVEN
**COMMUNICATION, COLLABORATION & STRATEGY**

# SHAWN BOYD
# MATT WISH

**MISSIONHIVE**
PUBLISHING

*MissionHive OS: An Operating System for Mission-Driven Communication, Collaboration & Strategy.*

By Shawn Boyd and Matt Wish

For permissions or inquiries, please contact hello@missionhiveos.com. To learn more, visit missionhiveos.com.

**Scripture quotations are from:**
The Holy Bible, English Standard Version® (ESV®), copyright © 2001 by Crossway, a publishing ministry of Good News Publishers. Used by permission. All rights reserved.

**Library of Congress Cataloging-in-Publication Data**
Boyd, Shawn and Wish, Matt.

*MissionHive OS: An Operating System for Mission-Driven Communication, Collaboration & Strategy / Shawn Boyd and Matt Wish.*

ISBN: 979-8-218-77650-3

**Subjects:**
1. Church Work—Leadership. 2. Church Management. 3. Communication in Church Work. 4. Christian Leadership—Teamwork. 5. Nonpro it Organizational —Management.

**Credits:**
Editor: Laura Boyd
Cover Design & Illustrations: Matt Wish
Interior Design: Sabir Robinson

# DEDICATIONS

To my wife, Laura, and our children, Savannah, Donovan, and Brooklyn—your presence in my life is a daily gift. Thank you for your love, your laughter, and the joy you bring to our family. You remind me every day what matters most. Your love and care means more than you will ever know. I am endlessly grateful to walk through life with you.

To my mom, who has always believed I could do anything and encouraged me to follow Jesus wherever He leads.

To the mentors, colleagues, and leaders who have challenged, inspired, and shaped this journey—thank you for your wisdom and partnership. Your insights and encouragement have left an indelible mark on this work.

To the ministries, leaders, and volunteers striving to live out your mission with clarity and purpose—you are at the heart of this book and the reason it exists.

To God, in whom we live, move, and have our being; who guides our path, gives us eternal purpose, and enables us to build His Kingdom—to You be all glory and honor.

**Shawn Boyd**

To my wife Bethany, who is out of my league in just about every way, thank you for seeing my potential and always encouraging me to reach for it.

To Patty and Michael (mom and dad), thank you for your endless prayers, sacrifices, support and for showing me what it looks like to let the Lord lead.

To all of my mentors, colleagues, leaders and friends who have walked through life with me. You remind me daily through your selflessness that nothing great is ever achieved alone.

Finally, to my sons, Jack and Finn and to the Next Generation of Christians, ministry leaders, pastors, planters, disciples, kingdom builders, and creatives—don't settle for the status quo. Be bold. Be brave.

And keep the mission first.


**Matt Wish**

# Table of Contents

# Part 1: Introduction to MissionHive OS

## Welcome to MissionHive OS

Think of your organization as a hive—a vibrant, mission-driven community where every individual plays an essential role in building something greater than themselves. In a healthy hive, every effort connects seamlessly, producing results that are sweet, lasting, and meaningful. But when the hive falls out of alignment—when communication breaks down or priorities shift—what was once a unified effort becomes fragmented. Honey isn't made, and instead, the hive is buzzing with activity but achieving little of lasting value.

If you're part of a faith-based organization—a church, ministry, or nonprofit—you've likely felt the thrill of seeing lives transformed through your shared mission. A new ministry program here, a volunteer recruitment drive there, a flurry of emails and meetings everywhere—and suddenly, the simplicity that once fueled your mission gives way to complexity. The harmony that once connected your team unravels, replaced by disconnected efforts, mixed messages, and a vision that feels harder to reach. Too often, this misalignment takes root when small shifts pull an organization away from the spiritual clarity that once guided its mission and purpose.

In a hive, every action—no matter how big or small—contributes to the greater good. Bees don't act in isolation; their work is guided by a shared purpose. Ministry is no different. When everyone—whether they're part of leadership, a ministry team, or a volunteer group—operates as one, aligned in purpose and clear in communication, the results are transformational: lives changed, communities uplifted, and faith proclaimed. Like a hive in harmony, every role seamlessly contributes to the shared mission. But when silos form or priorities clash, the hive falls out of alignment. The fruit of your labor—like the honey of a thriving hive—remains unrealized.

As you hold this book, you may know this tension well. Maybe you've experienced moments of joy as you've seen God move through your efforts—times when everything felt aligned, when lives were transformed, and your mission was crystal clear. And yet, perhaps you've also felt the frustration of working in a system that seems out of sync: communication strained, efforts duplicated, and the clarity you long for slipping out of reach. Whether you're a leader, team member, or volunteer, these challenges touch every part of an organization.

This is why we developed MissionHive OS—an operating system that mirrors the natural rhythm and goals of the hive while drawing on the principles of servant leadership. Just as a hive thrives when every bee is empowered to play its role, your ministry flourishes when its people are equipped and sent out to fulfill their God-given purpose. In the Bible, honey is a recurring theme; a delightful symbol of the sweetness that comes from pursuing life with God and each other. MissionHive OS seeks to align your effort with your mission, fostering this kind of unity and faithfulness. This framework prioritizes collaboration and trust, leaving room for God's Spirit to guide your organization's unique journey.

MissionHive isn't a rigid operating system where every action guarantees a fixed outcome. Instead, it nurtures cohesion and alignment while making space for the unexpected—for God to lead the way. It's not a "do A, get B" formula; it's a guide to position your organization for clarity and impact. Even if the path leads to "G" instead, you and your teams will be ready.

To bring these principles to life, we'll follow two fictional but true-to-life organizations facing challenges that mirror your own—revealing how MissionHive OS transforms confusion into clarity and activity into purpose. These stories show how real organizations move from fragmentation to alignment, bringing these principles to life.

In the chapters ahead, we'll explore what "real accountability" looks like in a culture of trust and collaboration, where alignment isn't just a line item but a living, breathing connection that unites your entire team. You'll discover a new view of mission-driven communication, where every person—whether a volunteer or senior leader—plays a meaningful role in keeping the mission alive and central. Each chapter will end with an "Aha" moment and a "Reflect & Apply" prompt for you and your team to start exploring these principles within your organization.

It's important to know that this is not a corporate model rebranded for ministry; this is a practical framework, purpose built from the ground up and designed for faith communities, rooted in the divine work God is already doing in and through you.

Welcome to MissionHive OS—a way to cultivate your mission with clarity, purpose, and a heart open to God's guidance.

With faith, love, and encouragement,

**Shawn and Matt**

CHAPTER ONE

# The Birth of a Vision

*"Where there is no vision, there is no hope."*

**George Washington Carver**

In every faith-based organization, there comes a point where good intentions collide with the reality of complex operations. For Shawn Boyd, a seasoned communications and operations professional, this point came repeatedly over the course of his nearly 30-year career. After navigating the worlds of business, global missions, and large church ministry, Shawn began to recognize a troubling pattern: *ministries, no matter their mission, size, or setting, often struggled with alignment, communication, and consistent purpose.*

But this realization wasn't sudden. It emerged gradually as Shawn encountered the same operational obstacles across diverse environments—from a bustling multinational missions organization to a rapidly expanding church back in the United States. Whether ministries were using business-oriented operating systems, adapting corporate models like the Entrepreneurial Operating System (EOS), or attempting to lead with traditional top-down organizational structures, he noticed recurring themes: *disjointed communication, a tendency toward silos, and a slow but steady drift from the core mission.* These weren't issues that could be solved with a few tweaks; they were systemic. And, as Shawn would come to realize, they required an entirely new approach.

Shawn's research revealed a significant gap: no operating system or framework was tailored to address the unique, mission-driven dynamics of ministries, nonprofits, and faith-based organizations. Systems designed for the business world often focus exclusively on leadership or efficiency, falling short in relational and mission-centered contexts. Attempts to adapt these systems to ministry environments frequently lead to frustration–not only because they fail to empower teams or foster alignment but because their underlying purpose and measures of success often conflict with the spiritual goals of ministry. At the same time, books covering leadership, organizational culture, communications, or change management typically exist as standalone works, forcing ministry teams to cobble together insights from disparate sources.

MissionHive OS seeks to bridge this gap by uniting staff at every level with a relational, mission-centered framework that equips them to align their efforts, communicate effectively, and pursue their shared calling with clarity and confidence. Unlike existing systems or books, MissionHive OS doesn't just focus on leaders but empowers every team member to contribute meaningfully to the organization's mission. While specialty resources may still have their place, MissionHive ensures the entire organization operates in harmony–on the same page, with the same purpose.

## The Journey Toward MissionHive

Shawn's journey toward creating MissionHive began long before he even conceived of it as an operating system. He grew up in the church, stepping into teaching and leadership roles as a young adult. Over time, God called him into full-time ministry, where he served as Global Marketing Operations Director for a large missions organization and later as Communications Strategist for a multi-campus church. Despite working with passionate teams and committed leadership, Shawn watched as these organizations grappled with communication breakdowns, often creating tension and inefficiency. Ministries that started with vibrant visions and noble missions found themselves bogged down by tactical overload, staff frustration, and a lack of coherent direction. God's mission was too often becoming veiled by busyness.

One defining experience came while Shawn was managing a multi-month initiative to build a marketing and communications (Marcom) knowledge base for a global missions organization. Here, he led training and workshops, diving into concepts such as Archetypes and journeys, all designed to help teams communicate more effectively. But no matter how well these ideas resonated with staff, he discovered that organizational structure consistently blocked true change. Think about that for a minute. Go back and re-read that last sentence. *Organizational structure blocked true change.* Top-down directives limited free-flowing communication, and tactical decisions preempted strategic vision. The insight grew clearer: if an organization's fundamental structure impeded communication and adaptability, then no amount of Marcom training or knowledge-building could fix the deeper issues.

This discovery led Shawn to pursue academic research, culminating in a master's degree in Executive Leadership. Combining practical experience with academic rigor, Shawn began piecing together a framework that would serve as the foundation of what would eventually become the MissionHive Operating System.

## Critical Realizations

There were several key realizations along the way. One such moment came through a profound insight in R. Mark Dillon's book, *Giving and Getting in the Kingdom.* Dillon's assertion that messaging in ministry should be about self-disclosure, not self-promotion struck a chord with Shawn. It shifted his perspective entirely: ministry messaging wasn't about flashy campaigns or catchy slogans—it was about truthfully revealing why the ministry existed in the world. It was about aligning with the mission, not manipulating it to achieve superficial engagement. It made room for "real world" Marcom tools but re-framed how and why they are used in a ministry context.

As he began incorporating this philosophy into his Marcom efforts, Shawn saw firsthand how the idea resonated deeply with ministry staff. This led to more focused conversations around purpose and the deeper meaning behind messaging. However, another reality soon surfaced: even the best mission-driven messaging couldn't thrive within an organizational structure designed around quantitative benchmarks.

This led to yet another significant realization: business operating systems that valued numbers over people—like the EOS framework— were ultimately misaligned with the relational, mission-focused work of ministry. Metrics, while useful, couldn't capture the transformational work of discipleship, community impact, or spiritual growth. Quantitative goals could easily overshadow qualitative, mission-aligned priorities, resulting in a church or ministry that appeared successful on paper but struggled to resonate with its people. If you're feeling, or have felt, that tension, you are not alone.

## The Ineffectiveness of Structural Approaches

Through both academic research and real-world experience, Shawn identified common organizational pitfalls:

- **Tactical-Driven Decisions Over Strategic Purpose:** Without a mission-centered framework, organizations relied heavily on tactics, often chasing immediate "doing" without understanding their deeper "why." Meetings focused on building task lists rather than planning strategic direction.

- **False Consensus Effect:** Organizations routinely made decisions assuming they understood their audience, yet frequently misread their actual needs. This led to poor hires, disengaged congregations, and an overall misalignment with the community's real concerns.

- **Unhealthy Cycles of Responsiveness:** Ministries often became overwhelmed with day-to-day tasks and tactical pursuits, creating an illusion of productivity that masked inefficiency and misalignment (Eyal & Lee, 2019).

- **High-Functioning Dysfunction:** Perhaps most insidious was a pervasive culture of "high-functioning dysfunction"—a state where everyone was busy but few were truly effective. Silos and fragmentation became the norm, and, even as individuals worked hard, little collective progress was made toward the guiding mission.

These discoveries highlighted that if ministries continued to rely on conventional operating models or top-heavy structures, they would remain in a cycle of frustration and inefficiency. What they needed was a new approach—a way to reframe organizational alignment, communication, and strategy around their mission.

## Partnering with Matt Wish

Meanwhile, Matt Wish was charting his own course in ministry marketing, with a career spanning both corporate and faith-based sectors. Growing up in a close-knit Christian community in West Michigan, Matt had long been involved in the life of the church, holding various volunteer and staff roles, from youth ministry to worship leading. After earning a communications degree, he began his career in corporate marketing, working with large brands and learning the importance of effective storytelling in marketing and advertising.

In 2019, feeling the need for more purpose-driven work, Matt founded Sonder Marketing in Southern California. His agency aimed to help organizations tell stories that connect, inspire, and create real change. The name Sonder itself represents the empathetic understanding that everybody has a complex and unique story of their own. Matt is driven to understand his clients story as well as their clients' stories so that meaningful connections can take place. Not just sales. Through his work with ministries and nonprofits, Matt noticed recurring issues that hindered their effectiveness, including what he termed "organizational entropy." Many ministries that began with a "you can do it, we can help" mentality would, over time, shift to a "we can do it, you can help" mindset. He identified a natural drift that often went unrecognized, and when finally noticed, it had usually set the organization back a number of years. Not to mention the mountain they faced when needing to earn back the trust of their audience. This shift underscored the need for a system like MissionHive OS, one that could reframe the relational dynamic between ministries and their people, keeping the mission at the center of all interactions.

Matt's experiences with multi-campus churches and large nonprofits showed him that ministries frequently lacked the strategic alignment needed for cohesive, effective communication. His work highlighted the need for an empathy-driven operating system—one that prioritized strong internal communication and alignment around mission rather than focusing solely on quantitative goals. He often noticed that ministry teams were overworked, underpaid, and believed that they were on mission, when in reality their heavy focus on measurable metrics had created misalignment and toxicity in the organization.

## The Convergence: MissionHive OS

It was during a period of overlap at the same multi-site church that Matt and Shawn first met. Matt had recently served as Communications Director, and Shawn was hired to lead strategic communications and planning efforts. Though their time together on staff was brief, their conversations quickly revealed a shared perspective: ministries often defaulted to tactical overthinking while starving deeper strategy. Their shared frustrations—and hopes—became a spark.

Outside of their day jobs, Shawn and Matt began developing what would eventually become MissionHive OS. Drawing on their individual experiences in ministry, global nonprofits, corporate strategy, and communications, they spent nights and weekends drafting and refining a new framework. These ideas weren't born out of formal assignments—they were born from passion, prayer, and a sense that God was inviting them to offer something better.

MissionHive OS emerged not as a reaction to one organization's challenges, but as a new approach for any ministry ready to shift from hustle to health, from tactical scrambling to aligned mission. In the chapters ahead, you'll see how this operating system took shape and how it can transform the way churches, nonprofits, and other faith-driven organizations lead their teams, steward their mission, and communicate with clarity and purpose.

### Aha Moment

MissionHive emerged from a pivotal realization: ministries are not businesses, and their unique, mission-driven work requires more than borrowed strategies or rigid hierarchies. While business operating systems may excel in efficiency and metrics, they often overlook the relational dynamics and spiritual purpose that define ministry. The breakthrough was clear—ministries need an operating system built to foster mission alignment, empower collaboration, and enable communication that flows freely at every level. MissionHive was born to address this gap, providing a framework that unites teams and focuses efforts on transformational impact rather than transactional goals.

### Reflect & Apply

Take a moment to reflect on the heartbeat of your organization. What are the primary reasons it exists? Are your day-to-day efforts more focused on checking off tasks or advancing your core mission? Consider where your organization falls on this spectrum and identify one or two specific areas where a stronger focus on mission could bring greater clarity and alignment.

# CHAPTER TWO
# Philosophy and Purpose

*"Understanding is the basis of care. What you would take care of you must first understand, whether it be a petunia or a nation."*
### Dallas Willard

Operating systems like EOS (Entrepreneurial Operating System) and traditional organizational structures promise order and efficiency, and in the corporate world, they work quite well. They offer ways to track concrete measurables and productivity. However, an operational framework that genuinely serves ministries must reflect their core mission and values—not just in strategy but in every interaction, goal, and decision. Efficiency cannot come at the expense of our purpose as a ministry. Each part of the ecosystem must complement the others.

In MissionHive, we call this operational ecosystem a *beecosystem*—a dynamic, interconnected organization where every member plays a vital role in advancing a shared mission. Like a hive, success depends on alignment: every bee knows its role and works in harmony with the rest. But alignment alone isn't enough. Just as each bee's unique role—gathering nectar, building the hive, or protecting the colony—is essential to the hive's survival, a thriving ministry requires empowering every individual to contribute their unique gifts and expertise. For the hive to thrive, every bee must have a role and a purpose in shaping and executing the work. Likewise, when people, processes, and communication come together in unity, the mission flourishes. The hive isn't just a metaphor—it's a model for how ministries can function at their best.

For Shawn and Matt, MissionHive represents more than just a response to broken or insufficient systems—it is an intentional alignment of communication, mission, and purpose designed for the unique dynamics of ministry-the entire beecosystem.

## Why Purpose Matters

Shawn and Matt's experiences highlighted a vital truth: ministries operate in a profoundly different environment than businesses. Success in the corporate world can often be measured in productivity metrics or profit margins, but in ministry, success is reflected in lives transformed, communities served, and relationships built. These can be very tricky "metrics" to track.

This is where it starts to get uncomfortable for a lot of ministry people. How many of us have struggled with the comingling of metrics and things like salvation? Weird isn't it? Celebrating salvations and baptisms and even attendance at a church or community event is not inherently bad, in fact those metrics can help gauge effectiveness or guide future strategy. But if you do the vision and strategy part first, then those numbers become living kingdom metrics and not just numbers on a spreadsheet or newsletter. MissionHive reflects these values, providing an alternative to models that prioritized efficiency over engagement and metrics over mission.

Ministries don't just need a framework for doing things right–they need one for doing the right things. And that means creating a system that holds mission at the center, every time.

Shawn and Matt realized the need for an OS that not only honored a ministry's mission but actively strengthened it. Ministries face unique challenges, balancing relational goals with operational needs. In these settings, the limitations of traditional systems quickly became apparent, leaving staff feeling disconnected, departments siloed, and communication fragmented. MissionHive addresses these issues by creating alignment without rigidity and by promoting accountability without excessive structure.

## Core Philosophy of MissionHive

The philosophy behind MissionHive is simple in theory yet transformative in practice. We offer three core principles as the pillars of MissionHive, each representing a critical shift from traditional operating systems:

1. **Mission-First Alignment**

    At its heart, MissionHive is built on the belief that mission must drive all organizational strategy and communication. Every decision, from strategic planning to resource allocation to messaging, should be grounded in the core purpose of the ministry.

Unlike models that focus on quarterly targets or departmental metrics, KPIs, OKRs, etc., MissionHive anchors goals in a mission that is steadfast and qualitative. Quantitative benchmarks have their place, but they don't define our purpose. Our purpose is the transformation of lives, the building of communities, and the pursuit of faith.

## 2. Relationship-Driven Communication Flow

MissionHive recognizes that ministries are inherently relational, and internal communication is key to nurturing these relationships. However, communication in many organizations is hampered by siloed structures and top-down flow. MissionHive counters this by creating a system for two-way communication that involves every structural level of the organization.

Through concepts like the Hive Effect, MissionHive enables ministries to foster connection, inviting feedback and aligning messaging in a way that is dynamic and responsive. This flow isn't just an operational tweak—it's the heartbeat of MissionHive, ensuring that alignment doesn't come at the expense of creativity or personal contribution. We will look at the Hive Effect briefly in this chapter but unpack it fully in later chapters.

## 3. Empowerment Over Control

Traditional systems often rely on rigid accountability structures, with clear top-down directives that limit innovation and personal engagement. MissionHive, however, emphasizes empowerment, giving each staff member the tools and freedom to make decisions that reflect the organization's mission and values.

By equipping people to understand the organization's core purpose and enabling them to communicate it effectively, MissionHive fosters an environment where staff feel both supported and empowered. This principle of empowerment is evident in every aspect of MissionHive, from Archetype development (which we will get into in much greater detail later on) to the strategic use of diagnostics and feedback loops.

These foundational pillars shaped MissionHive's philosophy, but they are only part of the story. Other insights and realizations helped refine the system, uncovering new ways to align ministries with their mission. Together, these discoveries create a comprehensive framework that addresses both strategic vision and day-to-day operations.

## Why and Who For

A key realization that shaped MissionHive was the critical distinction between *strategy* and *tactics*—terms often used interchangeably but that are fundamentally different. Strategy defines the overarching vision and long-term direction of an organization, while tactics are the specific actions taken to execute that vision. Confusing the two leads to scattered efforts and unclear priorities. Shawn saw this repeatedly: organizations allowing tactical decisions to dominate, sidelining strategic clarity, and leaving teams reactive instead of proactive. MissionHive addresses this by ensuring mission-driven strategy guides all actions, aligning every effort with the broader mission.

This challenge of aligning strategy and tactics is well-captured by Bernadette Jiwa, who emphasizes the importance of foundational clarity:

> "Until you do the hard work of understanding the 'why' and the 'who for,' every tactical 'how to' has the potential to take you down the wrong track. The most useful answers are the ones we take time to figure out ourselves—not the ones that everyone can find in a handbook" (Jiwa, 2014, 26).

Beyond strategy and tactics, another pivotal insight emerged from Shawn and Matt's understanding of the False Consensus Effect, introduced briefly in Chapter One. This psychological bias occurs when an organization's staff or leadership mistakenly assumes their own perspective reflects that of their audience. Operating in this "bubble" often leads to misaligned efforts and unmet needs. Recognizing this, Shawn incorporated Archetype development into MissionHive—a process designed to help organizations step outside their internal mindset and better understand the people they serve.

The consequences of the False Consensus Effect may feel all too familiar. Think about a meeting where a new initiative is pitched, and someone says, "Well, I wouldn't do that," or "I'd love that!" It's easy to assume our personal preferences reflect those of the audience. But this assumption often leads to disappointment and wasted effort. Archetypes provide a way to avoid this trap, enabling ministries to connect authentically with their communities while staying aligned with their mission. Taken a step further, ministry work, by its very nature, is selfless—centered on serving others. This means that when we're developing strategy or executing tactics, we must intentionally view every decision through the lens of those we are called to serve. Archetypes provide the clarity needed to shift from an inward focus to an outward one, ensuring that our work reflects the heart of the mission.

## The Hive Effect: Communication in Harmony

One of MissionHive's key innovations is the Hive Effect, a communication model designed to replace traditional top-down structures. In many organizations, communication flows in only one direction—leadership creates directives, and departments carry them out without opportunities for collaboration or feedback. As each team or region interprets the directive, silos are created because each team is executing their version of the initiative. Shawn and Matt recognized that ministries need a more adaptive and inclusive approach, one that values collaboration and reflects the relational focus of their mission without enabling silos to be created at all.

The Hive Effect operates as a dynamic system with three essential elements that mirror the interconnected nature of a healthy beecosystem.

At the top level, communication flows from the core Identity, anchoring the organization's mission and purpose. Like the queen bee in a hive, this Identity is not just a figurehead—it is the steadying presence that gives the hive its sense of unity and direction. If the queen is threatened or absent, the entire hive refocuses to protect and sustain her. Similarly, in ministries, our organizational Identity—anchored in our God-given mission and purpose—demands constant attention from every level. Without this focus, the hive's activities risk becoming misaligned, ineffective, or entirely abandoned.

At the bottom level, Archetypes represent the distinct roles and perspectives of the people served by and within the ministry. These Archetypes reflect not just who these individuals are but how they engage with the mission at different stages of their journeys. Much like the specialized roles of worker bees—builders, caretakers, and defenders—Archetypes embody the diversity of needs and contributions within the ministry. This ensures the organization meets people where they are, offering tailored communication and engagement without assuming a one-size-fits-all approach.

Connecting these two levels are the strategic Environments— spaces where alignment and engagement converge. These Environments are not just physical locations like churches or offices; they are the operational and relational hubs where mission, Identity, and Archetypes meet. Like the hive itself, Environments foster connection and action, providing the structure for ministry efforts to thrive while remaining flexible and responsive to changing needs.

Together, these three elements create the Hive Effect, fostering a two-way flow of communication that empowers organizations to remain mission-focused while dynamically adapting to their communities. Just as a hive thrives on harmony and purposeful activity, the Hive Effect ensures that ministries operate with clarity and connection, enabling them to navigate complexity without losing their shared purpose.

But communication is only part of the equation. For the Hive Effect to truly succeed, it requires every member of the organization to contribute, collaborate, and feel connected to the mission. A thriving ministry depends not just on structured systems but on equipping and empowering every individual to play a meaningful role.

## Everyone is a Collaborator

Shawn and Matt constantly emphasize the importance of *collaboration* over *control*. Silos and top-heavy hierarchies didn't just impede communication—they stifled creativity and engagement. In fact, Matt worked with a nonprofit that had eight people on staff. The organization was using the EOS system, with seven of the eight staff members on the Executive Leadership Team (ELT). Talk about top-heavy. This structure meant that their weekly L-10 meeting essentially became a full staff meeting, though notably, the graphic designer wasn't included. Not exactly the best way to make her feel part of a shared mission.

MissionHive OS (MHOS) recognizes the importance of operational structure but takes a distinct approach from traditional corporate hierarchies. It acknowledges that every team member—from the graphic designer to the executive director—is on staff not just for a paycheck but because they feel called to a shared mission by God. A graphic designer could "push pixels" anywhere, and likely for more money in a business setting, but they choose to use their God-given talents to serve a Kingdom mission. Ministries need a system that empowers staff without overwhelming them—one that fosters cross-departmental alignment while preserving each team member's role autonomy and sense of purpose.

As MissionHive took shape, it became clear that its principles weren't just philosophical—they were practical. Each time Shawn and Matt worked with churches and nonprofits to apply MissionHive's ideas in real-world contexts, the sessions affirmed their insights. These experiences validated MissionHive's core principles and inspired organizations to rethink their approach to mission alignment and communication flow.

Shawn and Matt hope that what you have read so far resonates with you no matter what title or level of hierarchy you hold in your ministry. The chapters ahead will dive deeper into the MissionHive philosophy through the lens of two organizations struggling to navigate these common challenges.

### Aha Moment

Shawn and Matt saw that communication had to be dynamic, a dialogue rather than a directive. For MissionHive, the real "aha moment" was understanding that mission alignment depended on fostering relationships—not just between the organization and its audience, but within the organization itself.

### Reflect & Apply

Reflect on the way communication flows in your organization. Is it primarily top-down, bottom-up, or both? Consider one area where greater collaboration and feedback could improve alignment with your mission. How might you begin introducing this in a way that encourages empowerment rather than control?

# Part 2: MissionHive in Action Case Studies

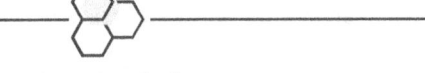

## Hive Insight

In this section, we'll follow the stories of two fictional organizations: Harvest Ridge Community Church (HRCC) and FaithLink Ministries, as they face real-world challenges that disrupt their mission and unity. For some of you reading, these case studies will hit close to home, and for some of you, you might think we are reading your mail. That's ok. We've created these case studies from real interactions across many organizations. These case studies bring us into the complexities of their operations, cultures, and goals, revealing the pain points that often arise when organizational structures clash with mission-driven ministry work. From Identity struggles to communication breakdowns, we'll see how both organizations encounter obstacles that feel insurmountable without a strategic, communication-centered approach.

Through these narratives, we invite readers to experience the limitations of existing structures and operating systems. While both HRCC and FaithLink bring heart and dedication to their missions, their struggles highlight a universal truth: without alignment around purpose and clear, consistent communication, even the most passionate organizations can find themselves disconnected and lacking effectiveness.

The aim of Part 2 is not only to introduce the need for an operating system like MissionHive but to foster solidarity with those in ministry who know these struggles firsthand. It sets the stage for MissionHive to step in as a solution that doesn't merely patch holes but establishes a framework where organizations can thrive, mission-first.

Before we dive into the narrative, let's introduce the cast of characters. You'll get to know each of them well in the chapters ahead, and you may even recognize aspects of yourself in their stories—or connect deeply with one or two. These characters are crafted as composite portrayals of real people serving in ministry roles at churches and nonprofit organizations.

## Harvest Ridge Community Church (HRCC)

HRCC is a 20 year old, multi-site church community in Colorado Springs, focused on fostering spiritual growth and relational connection among its members.

Originally a small, close-knit congregation, HRCC has expanded to two campuses, embracing structured growth while striving to retain its mission-centered, community-driven values.

**Pastor Greg Johnson - Lead Pastor**, originally envisioned HRCC as a spiritually mature, mission-driven community. Struggles with the church's shift toward metrics-driven operations and the feeling that HRCC is losing its relational depth.

**Michael Burke - Executive Pastor**, with a corporate background. Introduced the Entrepreneurial Operating System (EOS) to bring structure and efficiency to the church's operations, though he faces pushback about its effects on church culture.

**Kim Taylor - Family Ministries Director**, successfully manages an enthusiastic volunteer-driven ministry but feels increasingly isolated due to departmental silos and lack of cross-ministry alignment.

**John McCall - Communications Director**, tasked with managing internal communication but feels overwhelmed by conflicting departmental requests. Struggles to create a unified message that aligns with HRCC's core mission across all ministries.

**Jeremy King - Campus Pastor**, feels a disconnect in volunteer engagement and consistent attendance at HRCC's new campus, and notes the struggle to create consistent messaging and a sense of unity across campuses.

## FaithLink Ministries

FaithLink Ministries is an international nonprofit, headquartered in Colorado Springs, CO. FaithLink is dedicated to providing holistic, faith-based support to underserved communities worldwide through programs in health, education, and community-building. Founded with a mission to create sustainable change, FaithLink has grown to operate in over 30 countries, adapting its core initiatives to meet local needs while striving to maintain a unified vision

**Emily Roberts - Executive Director**, grapples with balancing regional autonomy with FaithLink's core mission and faces donor confusion due to inconsistent messaging.

**Maya Gonzalez - Director of Communications**, faces challenges in maintaining consistent messaging to donors and supporters across regions, which threatens the clarity of FaithLink's brand and mission.

**James Lawson - Director of Regional Operations for Africa**, appreciates the autonomy to adapt programs to local needs but feels isolated from the broader FaithLink family and sees the strain it puts on FaithLink's unified mission.

**Sarah Njoroge - Field Volunteer Coordinator in Kenya**, enjoys the impact of localized programs but feels disconnected from the larger organization and unsure how to communicate the broader mission to volunteers cohesively.

**David Carter - Senior Fundraising Officer**, notes that inconsistent messaging has confused longtime donors, impacting donor trust and funding stability.

## MissionHive OS

MissionHive is an operating system created to help ministries and nonprofits align their growth strategies with their core mission and values. Designed to support both structure and relational depth, MissionHive empowers teams to work collaboratively, ensuring that every department is unified in purpose and driven by the organization's foundational calling.

**Matt Wish - Cofounder**, helping HRCC and FaithLink realign with their core mission. Guides ministries to focus on relational, mission-centered growth while maintaining necessary structure.

**Shawn Boyd - Cofounder**, partners with Matt to help organizations like HRCC and FaithLink diagnose and address mission drift, fostering cohesion across departments through a strategic, mission-first operational system.

# CHAPTER THREE

# Reviving Hope: The Story of a Large Church's Transformation

*"God tends to bring renewal by starting new things.*
*It's the new wine, old wineskin concept.*
*It's easier to give birth than to raise the dead."*

**Alan Nelson**

Harvest Ridge Community Church (HRCC) began as a small, family-like congregation, where Pastor Greg Johnson could call each member by name. For years, their mission was clear and embodied by everyone who walked through their doors. However, as the church grew, so did its ambition. They expanded to two campuses and eventually, like many modern churches, hired an Executive Pastor, Michael Burke, who introduced a business-oriented framework: the Entrepreneurial Operating System (EOS). EOS promised to bring structure, allowing HRCC to reach more people and improve efficiency.

But two years into the EOS adoption, the cracks were becoming undeniable. Despite the increased structure, there was confusion, frustration, and a deepening sense of disconnect. HRCC had lost something essential in its pursuit of growth.

## The Identity Crisis

Pastor Greg felt it first. Originally, he had envisioned Harvest Ridge as a community church—grounded in relationships, service, and spiritual growth. The church's Identity statement was intended to guide their efforts, "Transforming lives, building communities, and spreading hope to the world." But with the implementation of EOS, metrics and numbers were now defining their success or failure. With EOS the staff began tracking "Rocks" which represent the specific, high-priority goals that an individual aims to achieve within a given quarter. They combined EOS with 4DX, a system that utilized lead and lag measures and also tracked Key Performance Indicators (KPIs). These KPIs focused heavily on attendance numbers, budget goals, and other quantitative data points that looked great on paper but that Greg felt didn't connect to HRCC's original mission.

"Are we becoming the type of church where growth has become our core Identity?" Greg asked his leadership team one afternoon. "We're growing in numbers, yes, but I worry that we're losing what makes us who we are."

Michael, who came from a corporate background working as an executive in the tech industry, reminded him that growth required structure. "If we're going to continue to serve our community effectively, we need to be organized. EOS brings us that organization."

Yet Greg's unease persisted. He sensed that the focus on numerical growth and efficiency was detracting from the church's Identity as a mission-driven, family of families.

## Silos and Hierarchical Disconnects

Across HRCC's ministries, a new challenge was brewing: silos. Departments were becoming rigid and isolated, working toward their own goals rather than collaborating on shared ones. The Children's Ministry was pushing its own initiatives, while the Worship Team focused solely on engagement metrics for weekend services. Kim Taylor, the Family Ministries Director, ran a successful ministry with enthusiastic volunteers, yet she felt increasingly isolated.

"It's like we're all on different teams now," she confided to John McCall, the Communications Director. "We used to feel like one church, and now it's like everyone's speaking a different language."

John, who bore the brunt of managing communications, felt similarly. With each department pursuing its own Rocks and priorities, he found himself mediating between competing interests. In fact, John had dropped communications team Rocks altogether because just about everything in the organization came across his desk anyway, which included other teams Rocks. He figured that by his team completing the requests accurately and on-time, his team was doing their part by helping everyone else achieve their goals.

Requests flooded in from all directions—each Campus wanted a separate newsletter; Outreach wanted more promotional materials; Family Ministries wanted social media coverage for every event. Sometimes the ministry teams just made their own marketing content without working with the Comms team at all. Without a unified strategy, communication became fragmented, and the congregation began to notice. In the end, Rocks were creating unwanted churn, leading to busyness that sapped energy from the mission.

"Our church isn't speaking with one voice," John told Greg. "People are confused. They're seeing one thing from Family Ministries, another from Worship, and they're left wondering—what exactly is our church about?"

## Communication Breakdown Across Campuses

When HRCC opened a second campus in a culturally distinct part of town, disparities in messaging and outreach became even more apparent. While the main campus in suburban Colorado Springs focused on traditional, family-centered events, the new campus tried to engage a younger, urban demographic in ways that didn't always align with the church's core Identity.

Jeremy King, the Campus Pastor, noticed that volunteer engagement at the new campus was low, and some members questioned HRCC's commitment to serving their neighborhood. Week after week someone was on the platform begging church members to serve in children's ministry, but service in the community just dropped off the radar. During a staff meeting, Jeremy shared his concern: "We're trying to reach everyone, but it feels like we're not really connecting well relationally with anyone." Turning to John, he asked thoughtfully, "Isn't that a communications principle? You can't be everything to everybody, right?"

The Communications team struggled to create unified messaging that resonated across both campuses. HRCC's mission statement and values seemed to fade amid the noise of different initiatives, with no clear thread tying them together.

## When Growth Feels Like Loss

For longtime members, HRCC's expansion created anxiety about becoming too impersonal, too corporate. They feared losing the familial closeness they had cherished. Greg sensed this unease in casual conversations and overheard comments after services.

"Are we just chasing attendance numbers now?" one congregant asked on an open mic during a vision night. "I joined this church because it felt like family. Now, I feel like I'm just a number, and you keep asking more from me. It seems like Harvest Ridge is now focused on becoming the biggest church in town, not "transforming lives, building communities, and spreading hope to the world."

Even among the staff, this sentiment resonated. Many missed the days when they were a single, united community. It wasn't lost on Pastor Greg that he had sent some of his key volunteers to help launch the new campus location, and the original campus was noticeably struggling to fill the gaps. But with EOS metrics driving their meetings and growth initiatives, they felt pressured to push for more–more members, more events, more achievements.

## Leadership Disengagement

As the executive team's focus shifted toward EOS-driven metrics and growth strategies, many frontline staff members felt disconnected. The church's mission and core values became mere talking points, overshadowed by operational objectives and quantitative benchmarks. The original vision of HRCC as a community-rooted, relational church felt like it was slipping away.

Kim and Jeremy, along with other church staff, began voicing their concerns, not in formal meetings but in private conversations. "We're a church, not a business," they reminded each other. Jeremy caught himself referring to his satellite campus as a franchise because he felt the push to "Ridgeify" his team. Yet their concerns felt sidelined in favor of measurable outcomes and financial goals in a spreadsheet.

John shared an observation with Kim, "Our mission statement has become lip-service. It exists on paper and in marketing and communications content, but it's no longer part of our DNA. Every team is living out their interpretation as they see it, and it's not just staff that notice it. Our members feel it, too."

Finally in one meeting, Pastor Greg in a moment of frustration and transparency shared his own fears. "I wonder if we've gained structure and become efficient but lost sight of our mission." The room fell silent. Slowly, staff members began to nod, acknowledging what many had felt but not dared to say out loud.

## A Church at a Crossroads

HRCC's journey reveals the tensions and fractures that can emerge when growth and efficiency take precedence over mission and Identity. Pastor Greg and his team had pursued a structured, metrics-based operating system to streamline operations and reach more people, but in the process, they lost sight of what made Harvest Ridge unique.

The church was growing numerically, but relational connections, unity, and mission clarity were slipping away. The staff felt disengaged, departments were siloed, and the congregation sensed the disconnect. They were feeling like the church was becoming wider but certainly not deeper.

Greg thought back to the early days of the church when they'd spontaneously baptize 20-30 people on a weekend and how exciting that was. How was that even possible without a website, live streams or social media? Nowadays the ministries were so siloed that after six months of designs and revisions, they couldn't all agree on what the baptism t-shirts should say.

As HRCC stood at this crossroads, Pastor Greg knew they had to make a decision. They could either double down on EOS and its metrics-driven approach or find a way to refocus on their mission and community-centric values.

Greg was hungry for a way to reorient HRCC around its core mission and relational values, allowing them to grow with purpose and clarity without sacrificing spiritual depth. However, he knew he needed help diagnosing the issues he could feel but couldn't articulate. He needed an outside perspective that understood the unique needs and challenges of a growing church. He began praying for God to provide direction.

## Aha Moment

For HRCC, tensions were becoming a wake-up call. They began to realize that their quest for growth and efficiency had unintentionally led them away from their foundational mission. The solution wouldn't be about abandoning structure but rather about finding a way to pursue both structure and relational, mission-first growth.

## Reflect & Apply

Consider whether your organization is chasing growth at the expense of its mission and values. Where do you see signs of misalignment? Are there areas where tactical goals might be overshadowing the "why" of your work?

# CHAPTER FOUR

# Mission Realign: Turning Points for a Nonprofit Ministry

*"We are called to be faithful, not successful."*

**Mother Teresa**

FaithLink Ministries, an international nonprofit organization, was founded on a clear and urgent mission: to bring holistic support to underserved communities across the world through faith-based programs, education, and community-building efforts. Headquartered in Colorado Springs, FaithLink had grown from a small local outreach into a global organization with operations in over 30 countries.

While FaithLink's expansion had been impressive, growth had brought unintended consequences. The organization was stretched thin, with each region adapting FaithLink's core initiatives to meet unique local demands. In doing so, however, they risked compromising their Identity and mission, creating fragmented services and inconsistent messaging.

This was the backdrop as Executive Director Emily Roberts faced mounting pressure from both staff and supporters. While some regional leaders praised the flexibility of adapting to local needs, others expressed concerns that FaithLink was straying from its original purpose and making up the mission as they went.

Emily knew the organization needed help. If they were to survive and thrive in their next chapter, FaithLink would need a unified approach—one that honored local contexts without sacrificing the core mission that had helped so many.

## Growing Pains and the Risk of Mission Drift

Emily had joined FaithLink as an intern in college during its early days, driven by a passion to support communities globally. As FaithLink expanded, she had managed to retain this vision, but she increasingly found herself balancing organizational growth against fidelity to their mission. With so many regional programs under the FaithLink banner, the original vision often seemed obscured by operational demands and regional pressures.

"I feel like we're a different organization in every country we work in," Emily admitted during a leadership team meeting. "We've allowed each region so much independence that our core reason for existence is getting lost."

James Lawson, the Director of Regional Operations for Africa, spoke up. "In our communities, we face unique needs that aren't always addressed by the programs designed at HQ. We need flexibility, Emily."

This dynamic wasn't unique to Africa. Across Europe, Asia, and Latin America, FaithLink's regions had developed distinct identities and operating styles. This adaptability had helped FaithLink become relevant in each context, but it came at a cost: the broader mission was increasingly fragmented, with local leaders unsure how to stay true to FaithLink's overarching values and purpose.

## Inconsistent Communication to Donors and Supporters

Donor engagement presented a similar issue. Maya Gonzalez, the Director of Communications, found herself working around the clock to manage the various requests from regional leaders and create tailored messaging that resonated with each area. In her mind this busyness and grind was just part of the deal in missional work. However, this piecemeal approach was taking a toll on the clarity of FaithLink's brand.

"We're sending out different messages to our supporters in every region," Maya explained to Emily in one meeting. "Our North American donors hear one thing, while European supporters get a completely different message. It's confusing, and frankly, it's weakening our credibility."

Maya had witnessed firsthand the challenge of keeping FaithLink's communications consistent while accommodating the varied priorities of each region. With each regional office speaking its own "language" to donors, Maya sensed a drift away from FaithLink's original calling.

FaithLink's Senior Fundraising Officer, David Carter, shared Maya's frustration. "We need to reconnect with our supporters around our mission," he said. "Right now, I'm getting questions from longtime donors who don't know what we stand for anymore."

One donor expressed their concern acutely when they called to stop their automatic donations, "There is no way one organization can effectively be all these things in all these places." Accurate or not, the perception was becoming negative.

Emily could see the issue taking shape: FaithLink had allowed its messaging to become as diverse as its programs. While regional teams were doing impactful work, the inconsistencies left supporters questioning the organization's core values.

## The Strain of Regional Autonomy

For James Lawson and his team in Africa, autonomy had been a blessing—allowing them to craft programs and communications that responded directly to their communities' needs. Yet, he admitted that with autonomy came challenges. He felt isolated from other regional leaders because FaithLink's strategies in Africa didn't always align with those in Asia or Latin America.

This feeling of separation was echoed by Sarah Njoroge, a Field Volunteer Coordinator in Kenya. "We're doing good work here," Sarah noted during a regional meeting. "But I feel disconnected from the larger FaithLink family. I have no idea what the organization is doing elsewhere, and I don't know how to communicate our global mission to our local volunteers. While they don't share the same concerns as donors, they want to know how their contribution locally contributes to what God is doing through FaithLink globally. Truthfully, I'm not in the loop to share anything valuable with them."

The struggle to maintain unity while allowing for local adaptation had created silos not only between regions but also between regional and headquarters staff. Each team was focused on meeting the specific needs of their communities, but the cumulative effect was a growing disconnection from the organization's collective mission.

FaithLink was at risk of becoming an organization of loosely connected parts rather than a cohesive whole. When staff advocated for FaithLink in public, they routinely opened with a phrase like, "Well, FaithLink is complicated." Maya and Emily were deeply concerned about this subtle but important reality.

## Confusion in Organizational Identity

The more Emily listened to her team, the more she realized that the central issue was one of Identity. FaithLink was founded to serve communities in a holistic, faith-centered way, but somewhere along the path of growth, that Identity had become diffused.

Emily wanted FaithLink to be known as an organization that brought comprehensive, Christ-centered support to underserved areas. But as she looked at the messages, programs, and reports coming out of each region, it was clear that FaithLink was communicating many different identities to different audiences.

Without a unified approach to define and reinforce FaithLink's core Identity, the mission was beginning to drift, leaving donors, partners, and even staff unsure of what FaithLink stood for.

"We need alignment," Emily concluded during a board meeting. "We're on the edge of losing who we are, and I won't let that happen."

## Setting the Stage for a Solution

Maya shared a reflective moment with the leadership team. "I think part of the frustration is that we know our mission is deeply valued, but the way we're operating sometimes makes it feel fragmented, like we're losing our voice. Maybe we're not the only ones in this position."

It was then that Emily recalled a conversation she'd had with Greg Johnson, the Lead Pastor of Harvest Ridge Community Church (HRCC). He had shared similar frustrations over fragmented communication, the strain of alignment across multiple locations, and the challenge of sustaining relational impact while pursuing growth.

Emily had learned about Matt and Shawn's work with the MissionHive

Operating System. As both HRCC and FaithLink faced similar challenges, she and Greg saw an opportunity for collaboration and reached out to the MissionHive team, hoping an outside perspective could help realign their missions without sacrificing operational health. The four quickly agreed on a joint consultation approach— an opportunity to surface root issues, share insights, and build a framework for moving forward.

### Aha Moment

For FaithLink, the turning point came when Emily recognized that allowing autonomy without unity had created a drift in their Identity and weakened their message. The solution would not be to restrict each region's independence but to offer them a balanced way to honor both the global and the local needs in their ministry.

### Reflect & Apply

Consider whether your organization's local adaptations or growth strategies are pulling you away from your core mission. Are there inconsistencies in how different teams or departments define and communicate your mission?

# Part 3: Diagnosing the Issues

## Hive Insight

Part 3 dives into the foundational work of assessing and diagnosing the core challenges that ministries face. This section brings together leadership teams from Harvest Ridge and FaithLink to confront their struggles with mission drift, fragmented communication, and structural silos. By focusing on each organization's "why" and "who for," these chapters explore the essential conversations that clarify purpose and bring to light the deeper challenges within each organization's operations. Through thoughtful, strategic questioning, Matt and Shawn guide both teams toward a renewed understanding of how tactical busyness often undermines true mission alignment.

These chapters set the stage for transformative change, as both organizations identify the relational and strategic gaps that have kept them from fulfilling their missions fully. You will see how confronting these core issues provides a foundation for the later implementation of MissionHive, demonstrating the power of mission-driven diagnosis as the first step toward genuine, lasting transformation.

# CHAPTER FIVE

# The First Steps–Assessing Reality

*"Great things never came from comfort zones."*

**Anonymous**

The conference room buzzed with a mix of anticipation and uncertainty as staff from HRCC and FaithLink gathered for their first joint assessment session. Long tables formed a square, allowing everyone to face one another—pastors, directors, and staff from all levels of each organizations' structural hierarchy were all in one space. Shawn and Matt stood ready to guide the two teams through a transformative conversation.

Greg exchanged a hopeful glance with Emily. Both had high hopes for what this collaboration could yield. They had realized that despite operating in different spheres—HRCC as a multi-campus church and FaithLink as a global nonprofit—their challenges bore striking similarities. Fragmented communication, mission drift, and a disconnect between their daily operations and core purpose plagued them both.

After opening in prayer, inviting God to work out His will in the days ahead, Matt addressed the room. "Thank you all for coming together today. We know how much commitment is required to be here together. James and Sarah—your willingness to fly here from Africa is not lost on us! You are both travel warriors." Turning back to the whole group, Matt continued. "Shawn and I believe that by sharing openly and engaging in honest dialogue, we can begin to uncover the root causes of the challenges you're facing."

Shawn added, "Our goal isn't to provide quick fixes but to guide you in rediscovering your organizational 'why' and 'who for.' As we answer those questions, we will also explore together how we can reshape the 'what' and 'how' of your daily operations."

## Unpacking the "Why": Rediscovering Purpose

Shawn gestured toward a whiteboard where the words *"Why do we exist?"* were written in bold letters. "Let's start with a fundamental question. For both HRCC and FaithLink, why do you exist as organizations? What is your core mission?"

Greg from HRCC was first to respond. Our mission statement is 'transforming lives, building communities, and spreading hope to the world.' By this, we mean that we exist to build a community of Jesus-followers who grow in their faith and impact the world around them. It's about discipleship and transformation."

Emily nodded. "For us, 'we exist to empower communities globally to create sustainable change in Jesus' name.' We aim to be catalysts for meaningful development and hope wherever God places us."

"Those are important missions," Shawn affirmed. "Do you feel that your daily activities and decisions align with these purposes?"

There was a pause before Greg reluctantly broke the silence. "Honestly, it doesn't always feel that way. We've been so focused on expanding our campuses and increasing attendance that sometimes the relational aspect gets lost. We have really wrestled with building a relational community and nurturing faith lately."

Jeremy King, the campus pastor at HRCC, added, "Our staff meetings are dominated by discussions on metrics— attendance figures, event participation—but rarely do we discuss spiritual growth or community impact."

Many around the table nodded in agreement, giving Jeremy the courage to pinpoint his own frustration: "Some of us call our staff meetings *'wins and spins'* because they feel more like a competition— who had the biggest event, the most baptisms, or whatever metric we're tracking that week."

Pastor Greg had heard this concern before and took it in stride. But following Jeremy's honest comment, a willingness for vulnerability settled over the room as both teams prepared to address their real issues head-on.

Across the table, Maya shared a similar sentiment. "At FaithLink, each regional office operates almost like an independent entity. Our communications are inconsistent, and it feels like we've lost a unified voice. We say we're empowering communities, but our fragmented approach might be hindering that very goal."

James chimed in. "We adapt central directives to fit our local context, but sometimes the original mission gets blurred. We're busy implementing projects, but I wonder if we're truly aligned with our core purpose. And since we are being really honest here, weeks can go by where I don't have a single 'Jesus conversation' with anyone. That bothers me a lot."

## Digging into Challenges

Wanting to engage this topic more deeply, Matt said, "It sounds like both organizations are experiencing a disconnect between your mission and daily operations. Let's explore why that might be happening. What factors contribute to this misalignment?"

Michael offered, "For us, adopting the EOS framework was meant to bring structure. But over time, it seems to have shifted our focus to internal efficiencies and numerical growth. The emphasis on top-down directives has made it difficult for feedback to flow upward, and I think that's part of the problem."

Noticing Jeremy's pleasant surprise at Michael's insight, Shawn nodded. "That's an important observation. How does top-down communication affect your team's ability to stay mission-focused?"

"It creates silos", John replied. "Departments become focused on their own goals and metrics, often losing sight of the bigger picture. There's less collaboration and more competition, even if unintentional."

Maya reflected on FaithLink's experience. "In our case, it means each region communicates differently. Headquarters sends out directives, but without considering regional nuances, the messages often miss the mark. There's little space or time made for strategic dialogue, so regional teams do their own thing. In fairness to them, they have a lot to do, and they are good at their work. But the disconnect is real."

"That leads to fragmentation," David added. "We're all working hard, but perhaps not all rowing in the same direction. The top-down approach doesn't allow for the local insights that could enhance our collective, global mission."

Matt asked, "Do you feel that this top-down communication style affects the 'who for'—the people you're serving?"

Jeremy responded immediately, "Absolutely. If we're not aligned internally, how can we effectively reach out to our congregation? Our messages become inconsistent, and people may feel disconnected or confused about our real motivations."

"For our beneficiaries, mission partners, and donors, inconsistent communication can erode trust," stated Emily. "If each region presents a different face of FaithLink, it becomes harder for them to understand who we are and what we stand for."

## Identifying the Impact of Misalignment

Shawn took a moment to summarize. "What I'm hearing is that both top-down communication and a focus on questionable metrics are contributing to silos and misalignment. This not only affects your teams but also the people you're serving—the 'who for' of your mission."

He continued, "Let's consider the consequences. How does this misalignment manifest in your day-to-day operations?"

John sighed. "There's a sense of busyness for busyness' sake. We're all working hard, but it doesn't always feel purposeful. Staff morale is affected, and I think our congregation senses it too."

Michael added, "We might be growing in numbers, but are we growing in depth? That's the question that keeps me up at night. And coming from the corporate world I'm seeing a difference in what stewardship means in a ministry context. It feels like our teams would rather be busy so they feel like they are contributing, but without a clear understanding of what they are contributing to, we are actually busy working on things that negatively affect our stewardship."

Shawn and Matt exchanged quick glances with raised eyebrows, recognizing Michael's commentary was remarkable.

Offering a FaithLink perspective, David shared, "Our donors sometimes receive conflicting messages from different regions. It creates confusion and can impact funding. Internally, staff may feel unsupported because they don't see how their efforts contribute to the larger mission."

## Reorienting Towards the "Who For"

Matt posed another question. "Given these challenges, how might refocusing on the 'who for' help realign your operations with your mission? By 'who for' I mean the people your organizations exist to serve."

Greg considered this. "If we prioritize the needs of our congregation— their spiritual growth, their sense of community— we might make different decisions. We might focus less on expanding for expansion's sake and more on deepening relationships."

"That could mean creating more spaces for genuine connection, adjusting our programs to meet people where they are, and listening more to their feedback," suggested Kim.

"For us, putting beneficiaries and local communities at the center could guide our regional strategies," Emily shared. "We could certainly do better listening to what the community needs rather than telling them what they will get. It would also encourage us to develop communications and programs that are more responsive and culturally relevant while still aligned with our global mission."

Maya agreed. "It might also mean establishing better feedback mechanisms so that local insights inform our organizational strategies, not just the other way around."

## Recognizing the Need for Change

Shawn looked around the room. "It seems we're arriving at a critical understanding. By shifting focus from internal metrics and top-down directives to the people you serve, you can begin to realign with your core mission."

Matt added, "This doesn't mean disregarding structure or efficiency. It means ensuring that these elements serve your mission, not the other way around."

"But how do we begin to implement this shift?" Michael asked. "It's one thing to recognize the need; it's another to enact change. It feels like we're making a leap already."

Shawn smiled. "That's the journey we'll embark on together. But first, it's essential that everyone here understands and buys into the 'why' behind the change you need. Without collective ownership, any new system or strategy will face resistance."

Looking at her team, Emily said, "I think we're ready. We can't afford to continue on this path if it means compromising our mission and the people we aim to serve."

Michael agreed. "Our communities deserve better. If changing our approach can enhance our mission, then it's worth pursuing. This has been a helpful conversation so far, but I want to know more."

## The Path Forward: Building Readiness for Transformation

Matt concluded the opening session. "This first discussion was about assessing reality—confronting the challenges honestly and understanding their root causes. The next steps will involve exploring how to realign your organizations strategically and operationally."

Shawn added, "But remember, transformation isn't a quick fix. It requires commitment, openness to change, and a willingness to rethink long-held practices. Are you prepared to take that journey?"

Heads nodded around the room. The leaders of HRCC and FaithLink felt a renewed hopefulness and a cautious optimism. The road ahead was not yet clear, but they now had a better understanding that the issues they faced were more common than they thought. Every staff member benefitted from hearing their counterparts and colleagues express their insights and assumptions. They were off to a good start.

### Aha Moment

By confronting foundational challenges and refocusing on the core mission (why) and those they serve (who for), organizations can begin to reimagine their operations and communications, paving the way for meaningful transformation.

### Reflect & Apply

Reflect on your organization's current focus. Are internal metrics and top-down communications overshadowing your mission and the people you serve? Identify one specific area where refocusing on your "why" and "who for" could initiate positive change.

## CHAPTER SIX
# More Dialogue: The Problem of Organizational Hierarchy

*"But Jesus called them to him and said, "You know that the rulers of the Gentiles lord it over them, and their great ones exercise authority over them. It shall not be so among you. But whoever would be great among you must be your servant, and whoever would be first among you must be your slave, even as the Son of Man came not to be served but to serve, and to give his life as a ransom for many."*

**Matthew 20:25-28**

The first assessment session with HRCC and FaithLink had surfaced powerful realizations. Now, the focus would turn toward the broader question of organizational hierarchy: how top-down systems, even well-meaning ones, inadvertently restrict engagement, foster silos, and cause team members to lose sight of the mission.

After a coffee break, the group reconvened.

"We're all in this room because each of you sees the potential for something better," Shawn began. "In this session, we're diving into the heart of why structural hierarchy, no matter how well intended, can disconnect us from the mission and, more critically, from the people we serve. The operating system that Matt and I designed is called MissionHive for a reason. Honeybee hives in the natural world provide a tremendous metaphor for healthy ministry operations. Everything in a hive, from its physical design, to the unique role of every bee, to the honey produced, all exists with a singularity of purpose achieved through mutual cooperation. We will go into depth on the hive metaphor as we move forward in these workshops, but it is critical that you understand we are taking you on an intentional journey of discovery–covering a lot of things–that ultimately must work together for your ministry to achieve its mission. Our view of structure is a key element of this design."

Matt continued, "It's easy to think that structure is the solution to all alignment problems. But structure can sometimes add layers that obscure the mission, preventing team members from feeling empowered to speak up or take ownership. In some cases, we try to solve challenges by hiring more people–but if they remain siloed–new staff don't solve the problems either. In fact, they likely create new silos. Let's open up space today to explore how hierarchy has shaped the dynamics in your teams and how that might be reimagined for greater mission alignment."

## HRCC's Experience: Top-Down Goals vs. Relational Ministry

Pastor Greg Johnson of HRCC followed Matt's lead first, visibly reflective as he spoke. "As HRCC grew, we thought that depending on our structure would help us stay aligned. But what I see now is that the approach we adopted–shaped largely by EOS–has shifted our focus from mission alignment to output and productivity. EOS leans heavily on top-down mandates, but I think our leadership team has been designing those mandates in an echo chamber without the feedback and insights of our entire staff. Alignment at Harvest Ridge now means following executive orders with a minimum of ownership in the implementation. That's not how Jesus empowered people, and I'm increasingly uncomfortable with our current direction."

He paused, acknowledging his Campus Pastor, Jeremy King. "Jeremy and his team have brought up time and again how they feel that the pressure to meet numbers is at odds with building genuine relationships. Our staff are spending more time working toward goals than with the people we're here to serve."

Jeremy nodded, adding, "And I'll say this because it's come up in our staff meetings and our volunteer discussions–there's a sense that our goals are serving a few leaders' goals more than the congregation. Volunteers, in particular, have started to feel like they're part of a machine, not a community. They want to connect, to be known and valued, but the structure we have in place doesn't create space for that."

Matt turned to Jeremy and nodded, acknowledging the weight of his insight. "It's powerful that you're aware of these issues, Jeremy and Greg. Many organizations go years without realizing the impact that top-down goals have on relational work."

Shawn shared an observation that HRCC was caught in a circular loop. To justify a new campus, the focus had shifted to securing the necessary people and funds for launch and sustainability. Once those were secured, top-down control and quantitative metrics rooted in HRCC's business-oriented operating system began to center on the wrong measures rather than the stated mission. This was creating an environment where relationships took a back seat to keeping the machine running smoothly from the top down.

## FaithLink's Hierarchical Disconnects: Regional Challenges

Matt invited FaithLink to offer their perspective on how hierarchy was shaping operations. James spoke next, sharing a distinct yet parallel issue. "One of the most significant challenges we face is the distance between HQ and the field teams. Every region has unique cultural nuances that don't always translate back to headquarters. We end up following directives that may look good on paper but don't work efficiently or effectively in our context."

He continued, "For example, our field staff in Kenya recently highlighted how difficult it's been to get community buy-in for a program focused on technology training. Headquarters saw this as a way to empower young people. But in rural areas, where resources are limited, families prioritize immediate needs. So, while we're meeting our program goals, we're not necessarily meeting the community's needs. And the cost to build the infrastructure is so high we don't have the budget to carry out the directive. There was clearly a disconnect between the HQ and our field realities."

Sarah spoke up, wanting to be careful she did not dishonor her leadership but realizing her perspective was needed. "When our field volunteers overheard us struggling with how to implement the technology directive, they were dismayed with how poorly it was planned. Even if we could build the infrastructure, rural Kenyans don't have the knowledge needed to train others. It was a bit of an embarrassment that took a considerable amount of my time and energy, I am sorry to say."

Maya then shared her perspective on how these top-down decisions affected her team's ability to communicate effectively. "Our Communications team often feels like they're delivering messages that don't fully resonate with people on the ground. We're sending out newsletters and updates, but we don't always capture what's really going on in each region. There's a lot of great work being done, but the stories we tell are missing the heart of it. And now hearing from James and Sarah, I am mortified how we presented the technology initiative to our donors." She looked at Jeremy before continuing, "It feels yucky—like one of the wins and spins you mentioned earlier."

Matt and Shawn could see that the discussion was revealing deeper tensions. They knew it was time to guide the conversation toward the underlying reasons why these challenges persisted.

## The Root Cause: Structure vs. Purpose

Shawn addressed the group, drawing out the connections between their stories. "What I'm hearing, from both HRCC and FaithLink, is that while hierarchy and structure are meant to create efficiency, they often prevent healthy alignment. Executive directives can overshadow the 'why' behind what you're doing."

He turned to Jeremy, "Jeremy, when you mention that your volunteers feel like they're part of a machine, that's a red flag. It suggests that they don't see themselves as a meaningful part of the mission. And, James and Sarah, your story about Kenya highlights a similar issue. When directives come from a distance—literally or figuratively—it creates a disconnect that can hinder relational work."

Matt added, "To move forward, we'll need to create ways for every person, at every level, to understand and contribute to the mission without feeling buried by hierarchy. Mission-aligned structure isn't about removing all control or accountability, but rather empowering people to take ownership of the mission in the role they have been entrusted to carry out."

Shawn continued, "Alignment with the mission can't be achieved through structure alone. It's about creating a system that allows voices from all levels to inform the way you communicate and engage. HRCC, you use EOS to guide you. FaithLink, you use hierarchy alone to guide you. Isn't it interesting that both "systems" lead to the same complicated issues?"

Matt began to transition toward a solution. "In MissionHive, we talk about the importance of a two-way flow of information. Hierarchies where the top-down approach dictates everything risk silencing the very voices that bring the mission to life. The challenge, then, is how to create a culture that allows this two-directional dialogue to shape the entire mission."

## Reframing Accountability: Empowerment over Control

Shawn led the group into a reflective exercise. "Imagine a ministry where accountability is more about ownership than control. Think about what would change if each of you–at any level of the structural hierarchy of your organization–felt empowered to make decisions based on the mission, rather than just following directives."

Jeremy considered this, thinking back to his conversations with volunteers. "I think it would change a lot," he said slowly. "If our volunteers felt like they had a stake in the mission—rather than just completing tasks—they'd feel more engaged and valued."

James chimed in, "For FaithLink, that would mean encouraging our field teams to make decisions based on local needs and trusting them to carry out the mission in ways that are contextually relevant. Of course, this would also mean that HQ consults our field teams when designing strategies so they get critical perspectives that shape the initiative from the beginning."

Matt and Shawn exchanged a glance, seeing the transformation taking place. Shawn responded, "What you're describing is what we call empowerment-driven accountability. Instead of hierarchy dictating every move, we should align everyone around the mission and give them the opportunity to contribute meaningfully from the earliest formation of strategy. That's where real change begins. Much of what you are dealing with involves putting tasks and checklists ahead of strategic collaboration. After lunch, we will dive into this topic."

### Aha Moment

The leaders from HRCC and FaithLink were beginning to see that structure and hierarchy, as they had been using them, were not sufficient for healthy mission alignment. They recognized that empowerment—at every level—could foster greater engagement and a stronger connection to the mission.

## Reflect & Apply

Reflect on your own organization's structure. How much of it promotes genuine mission alignment, and where does it simply reinforce control? Consider one area where you might shift from a top-down directive to an empowerment-driven approach, allowing team members to take ownership.

# CHAPTER SEVEN
# Understanding "Strategy Before Tactics"

*"Without counsel plans fail,*
*but with many advisers they succeed."*

**Proverbs 15:22**

Following a lunch break filled with lively discussion about the morning sessions, both HRCC and FaithLink's teams gathered again, anticipation mixed with a growing openness to change. The previous conversations had begun to unearth some of the deeper challenges each organization faced: mission drift, fragmented communication, and over-reliance on directives rather than strategic collaboration.

Shawn opened the session, setting a tone of clarity and purpose. "We're going to look more closely now at how a unified strategy can help you overcome the challenges we have been spotlighting today. Without strategy, you're left with isolated goals and siloed efforts that don't build toward the bigger mission. We need to dig into how strategy can align and empower your teams naturally, rather than relying on command and control approaches."

He glanced over at Greg Johnson. "Greg, you mentioned the heavy emphasis EOS places on metrics and meetings. What would you say is the primary focus of those meetings? Are they about detailed planning and strategic vision, or are they more about building task lists?"

Greg responded, "Honestly, it feels like the latter. We're always measuring, tracking, and updating. But it's become a cycle where there's little room for strategic reflection, or even emotional response. It's become very formulaic. The EOS meetings keep us busy, but they don't necessarily help us stay connected to the bigger picture."

Shawn nodded. "This is a common issue. When meetings are focused on task-checking, they often leave little room for asking deeper questions. Without time set aside for big-picture alignment, everyone ends up interpreting goals individually, leading to mission drift and reactive tactics."

This struck a chord with Kim and John from HRCC, especially after a recent incident: just weeks earlier, a part-time admin at Jeremy's campus had sent a mass email to over 2,000 people requesting kids' ministry volunteers—without consulting anyone on staff. She had heard in a staff meeting that the children's ministry was closing classrooms on Sundays because there weren't enough volunteers for every age group. Because tactics trumped strategy in HRCC's culture—starting with leadership but extending to part-timers and volunteer leaders— she did the first thing she thought of to try and help. It was hard for Kim and John to be upset with her. This approach seemed like her best opportunity to contribute directly to the mission. But this wasn't her responsibility and people who received the email were upset because it was a communication outside subscribed channels. Their frustration resulted in numerous complaints and spam flags. Kim had been working on a plan, but this situation was a setback.

Matt joined in, "That's a key reason why MissionHive emphasizes strategy before tactics. Task-driven meetings feel productive in the moment, but without strategy to guide them, they quickly lose alignment with the mission. Over time, we develop cultures in our ministries that become ad hoc and reactive—as demonstrated by the part-time admin. Strategic planning, by comparison, gives every action purpose and a connection to the bigger 'why.'"

Matt shared another quick example to drive the point home. "I once worked with an organization that introduced 15-minute meetings, hoping shorter sessions would force efficiency and keep everyone on task. But it never really worked. Why? Because they were addressing the symptom, not the root cause. The real issue was their habit of prioritizing tactics over strategy. Without fixing that underlying problem, no amount of time-saving tweaks could make their meetings truly effective.

## The Role of Strategy in Building Trust, Unity, and Discernment

Matt continued, "What we're looking at here isn't just about making tactical improvements. A well-constructed strategy has to support unity, cooperation, and trust across every part of the organization. When strategy is clear and empowering, it creates organic alignment without controlling every single move. This is where hierarchy alone can fall short—it can create structure, but without mission-aligned strategy, it often leads to rigid control rather than genuine empowerment."

Shawn followed up, "When everyone's working toward what they think is right for their own role, it can create unintentional drift and even mistrust. Strategy, if developed well, should be the invisible thread that connects everyone. It doesn't limit you; it frees you to work with others because you're moving in the same direction."

He turned to Maya Gonzalez. "How would more strategic clarity help in your regional communications?"

Maya responded thoughtfully, "Honestly, it would relieve a lot of pressure. Without a unified strategy, each region has felt the need to adapt messaging on its own. We've been doing what we think is best, but we end up with different interpretations of the mission. That can create confusion, especially for our partners."

"Do you have a recent example?" Shawn asked.

"Going back to the technology initiative in Kenya, the Africa team was building messaging focused on meeting infrastructure supply needs; while here in the US, we were already telling donors the project was up and running. At HQ we didn't understand how difficult the mandate was for them. Instead of firing up a few computers like we expected, they had to first find appropriate computers that could handle the software that they also needed to source, and then they had to train the trainers. We thought the initiative was going to be about basic administrative software training for the local rural community, but the developing technology sector in Nairobi gave the team opportunities to train young people in more sophisticated systems than we had imagined. They envisioned training their strongest disciples and sending them to the capital to be messengers of hope while generating a great income. We had no idea at HQ that there was this much disconnect, and our communication with donors was way out of touch. An initiative came down and was being executed in the region, but we were all on different wavelengths. With the best of intentions, of course. The region made a good idea a great idea, but the scope of needs was massively different."

Shawn smiled at Maya's insights. "Great example. I can see how that was frustrating to teams on both sides of the Atlantic. Despite everyone believing the initiative was clearly understood, poor communication at the planning phase caused some friction. This highlights an important point. Even a strong, purpose-centered strategy doesn't dictate every move but leaves room for tactical issues if communication is not two-directional and collaborative. Strategic collaboration allows each region or ministry to adapt to the shared mission only if it is well defined. If the executive team heard from the Kenyan team during the planning phase, someone could have said, 'No, that is not going to work like you think.'"

## The Power of Saying "No" as Mission Protection

Matt spoke with a serious tone, emphasizing a critical aspect of MissionHive: the empowerment to say "No" when something doesn't align with the mission. "One of the most liberating aspects of a clear strategy is that it gives you the confidence and authority to decline activities that don't serve the mission, or to question if the suggested pathway is the best way forward. When everyone knows the mission, every staff member—from the top down to the frontline—should feel empowered to protect it."

Emily looked thoughtful. "It sounds simple, but that would be harder than you make it sound. There are always things that seem important or that others want us to prioritize."

Shawn agreed. "Exactly, and that's where strategy-based discernment comes in. By aligning around a shared mission, you're not just free to say 'No'—you're called to do so when something doesn't align with your overall mission. In the long run, saying 'No' can be more powerful than saying 'Yes' because it preserves focus, resources, and energy for what truly matters."

Jeremy jumped in, "I see, it's like guarding the mission, right? You're setting boundaries that keep everyone focused on what we're actually here to do."

"Yes," Shawn replied. "Think of it as creating protective borders around the mission. Without this ability to push back, ministries quickly become overwhelmed by well-meaning but off-mission tasks, programs, or goals. That's how drift begins—small, seemingly good ideas or actions that slowly pull you off course. It's like a bee hive losing its temperature balance. Worker bees instinctively sense when the hive is too hot or too cold and adjust by fanning their wings or clustering together. Without that shared responsiveness, the hive can't survive. Similarly, in an organization, if teams don't push back or course-correct when misalignment starts, the mission can suffer. Collaboration and intentional action, like the bees' adjustments, are what keep the organization healthy and focused."

"Finally," Jeremy exclaimed as he raised his fists in the air with delight. "The hive metaphor has taken the stage!" Everyone laughed, breaking the serious tone that was building in the room.

## The Freedom and Responsibility in Alignment

Matt picked up the thread, speaking to the tension between empowerment and responsibility. "In MissionHive, alignment isn't about rigidly following orders; it's about everyone understanding the mission so well that they can work with autonomy that remains collaborative. Saying 'No' to the unnecessary allows you to say 'Yes' to what matters, with clarity and purpose."

James nodded, "This would make our teams more intentional, I think. Right now, there's a feeling of constantly chasing things without a clear filter."

Shawn added, "Exactly. And the clarity of your mission becomes the filter, not just for big decisions but for daily actions. Imagine what it would mean for each person to know that they can say 'No' confidently if something doesn't align. It's a responsibility, yes, but it's also the freedom to work with authenticity and purpose."

While it was great that the team was picking this up, both Pastor Greg and Michael were visibly a little uncomfortable. Matt picked up on it and asked them if this created any tension or concern from them.

Greg answered first, "In principle I love this. Seems like under ideal conditions it should work perfectly, but we don't always have ideal conditions."

"Can you unpack that?" Matt asked.

"I mean we try to hire well, bring in people who want to be on mission, but in any organization you have people who just see this as a paycheck. I hate to say it, but there are people who, when given the chance to say no, might abuse it. This risks creating conflict on a regular basis."

Matt nodded thoughtfully, recognizing the concern. "I get it, Greg. The reality is, no system is foolproof, and there will always be those who don't fully buy into the mission or alternatively can become overly critical. But that's where the culture we build becomes crucial. If we're clear on our purpose and continually reinforce it, alignment becomes something people naturally want to protect—not something they feel obligated to follow."

He paused, letting the idea settle. "It's less about giving a free pass to say 'No' and more about cultivating a team that understands why they'd say 'Yes' or 'No.' When everyone is rooted in a shared mission, decisions—big and small—start reflecting that purpose. And sure, that might mean setting boundaries with people who aren't fully aligned, but it also means we're empowering those who are passionate about the work to bring their best."

After hearing all of this Michael added, "So, it's really about giving people the tools and trust to make mission-focused decisions, while still holding the whole team or an individual accountable to that standard?"

"Exactly," Matt replied. "We're creating a framework where people are both empowered and responsible, where they understand the impact of their choices on the mission. It's freedom with accountability, not freedom without direction. In a collaborative culture, we are looking out for one another like the bees in the hive. If we only see a "No" as criticism and not as protection that keeps us mission-focused, we have to work on our culture of trust."

"The reality is—and we've seen this time and again—that implementing MissionHive often reveals when someone might not be the right fit for their role, or perhaps even for the organization as a whole," Shawn said. "And that's okay. Similar to the "right person right seat" concept in EOS, MissionHive provides you and your team with the opportunity to thoughtfully support these individuals, helping them find the right place, whether that's within your organization or beyond."

## Highlighting Strategy's Role in Reducing Control and Fostering Ownership

Matt recentered the group, his voice direct but encouraging. "A strategy that truly aligns with your mission will create a culture of trust, where ownership flows naturally. You don't need to micromanage or keep people under constant scrutiny. Instead, people understand why their work matters, and they take ownership because they see how it serves the bigger mission."

Shawn added, "In fact, when strategy is leading, you'll find that top-down controls change significantly. People operate with a greater sense of freedom because they're aligned and empowered, not micromanaged. The role of senior leaders will always have a controlling function, but it should be centered on guiding the overall mission and not the day-to-day activities."

Matt shared, "Alignment allows you to accomplish the same level of coordination without micromanaging. Imagine if every staff member at Harvest Ridge and FaithLink understood, without a doubt, how their role directly supports the mission. How would that change your daily operations?"

Emily responded, "It would take so much pressure off. It's exhausting to feel like we're constantly adjusting our work to meet ever-changing expectations. A clear strategy would give us the confidence that we're on the right path."

Shawn closed with a powerful insight. "When strategy is truly understood and owned by everyone, the 'what,' 'when,' and 'how' become secondary. They flow naturally from the 'why' and the 'who for.' And that is when true transformation happens—not just within the organization but in the lives of those you serve. Tactics must serve the strategy with a high-level of intentionality. If we jump to tactics without being strategic in our planning and communications, we are just falling into the trap of being busy in our silos that feel safe and familiar whether they are meaningful to the mission or not."

"And with that," Matt proclaimed, "we are calling it a day. Go home and get some rest. Tomorrow we will begin showing you how MissionHive offers solutions to everything we uncovered today. Let me close us in prayer."

**Aha Moment**

The realization that strategy must guide tactics to foster unity, trust, and natural alignment is a powerful one. Control gives way to empowerment when everyone understands and internalizes the mission. Two-directional communication plays a central role in strategic collaboration that should not be underestimated.

**Reflect & Apply**

Reflect on a recent decision or action within your organization. Was it guided by a clearly defined strategy, or was it reactive? Consider how a well-aligned strategy could reduce silos and improve cooperation in your team.

# Part 4: Core Components of MissionHive

## Hive Insight

In this part, we unpack the foundational components of the MissionHive framework, diving deeply into how each element of the Hive Effect-Identity, Archetypes, and Strategic Environments—work together to enhance communication, ensure alignment, and increase ministry effectiveness. Through a combination of core principles and real-world applications at Harvest Ridge Community Church and FaithLink, each chapter provides practical insights on aligning every aspect of the organization to serve its mission and community more effectively. As each component is explained, readers will begin to see how MissionHive brings clarity, adaptability, and relational strength to ministry operations.

# CHAPTER EIGHT

# Deep Dive into the Hive Effect

*"Strategies are not something you hope for;
strategies are something you work for."*

**Peter Drucker**

The group gathered again the following morning, with both the Harvest Ridge and FaithLink teams eager to dive into the MissionHive philosophy. It was the perfect setup for Shawn and Matt to unpack the Hive Effect, a system they believed would address many of the underlying tensions from yesterday's sessions.

Shawn began, addressing the entire room. "Today, we'll cover a framework that allows everyone in the organization to stay aligned with the mission without stifling creativity or initiative. It's not about centralizing control but about creating clarity, cooperation, and a sense of shared ownership and empowerment."

The room grew silent, the weight of these words settling over the group. HRCC and FaithLink had long been accustomed to top-down directives. The idea that information and alignment could flow dynamically was both intriguing and a little unsettling, even in light of the issues and pain points they had uncovered together. It felt like a tipping point moment.

Matt took the lead. "Think of the Hive Effect—a deliberate, two-way flow of information that aligns everyone with the mission but still respects the unique roles within the organization. It's about embedding a shared understanding of 'why' and 'who for' into every level of communication and activity. This model is less about changing anyone's role and more about reshaping how each person contributes to the mission. To understand this properly, we will finally dive into the metaphor of the beehive."

Jeremy let out a buzzing sound, mimicking a bee, and everyone laughed.

## Starting with Organizational Identity: Anchoring Communication in Purpose

Shawn introduced the first level of the Hive, Organizational Identity. "At the very top, we start with the 'why'—the core mission and purpose of the organization. This Identity is what defines everything below it and ensures that every message aligns with a shared mission."

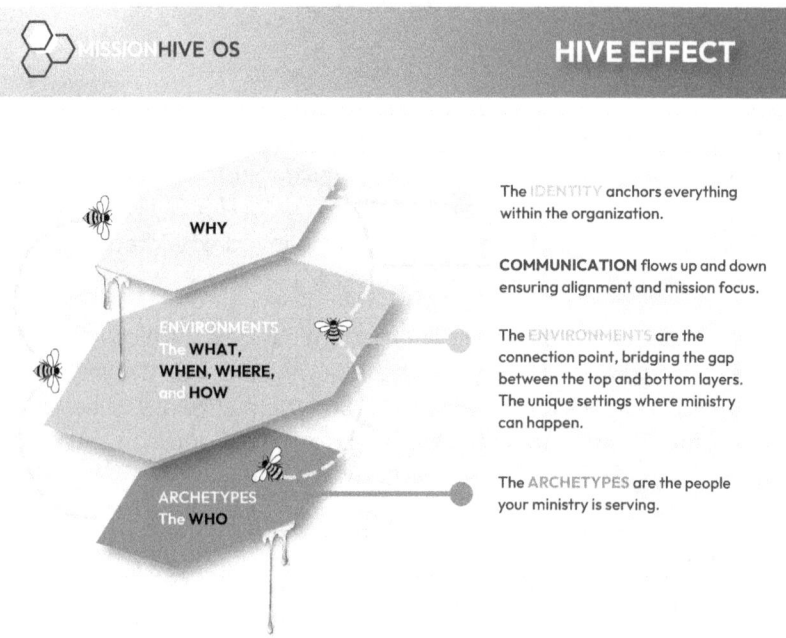

"Again, think of your organizational Identity as the queen bee," Shawn added. "She's not a micromanager directing every bee's movement, but her presence gives the hive its unity and purpose. When the queen is healthy, the hive thrives. But if she's absent or in danger, everything shifts—every bee reorganizes to protect and sustain her. That's how critical Identity is to your organization—it requires constant focus and alignment at every level. Before anything else, your Identity—whether you call it mission, vision, or purpose—is priority one. It is the unique and noble role God has given you in this world."

Pastor Greg nodded, recognizing this as a challenge they'd faced at HRCC. "So, if our Identity is about fostering relationships and discipleship, every piece of communication should reflect that purpose?"

"Yes, and more," Shawn affirmed. "When the Identity is clear and deeply embedded, it becomes the guiding force for every decision whether that is messaging, activity planning, or new strategic initiatives. It's about making sure that everything–every meeting, every ministry, every event–reinforces why you're here and who you're here for."

Emily raised a question. "And this is consistent across all departments and regions? Our teams often adapt messages to fit local needs, and that can sometimes stray from the core."

"That's a great point," Matt replied. "And this is where the Hive Effect works in your favor. While the core Identity remains the same, the way it's expressed can be contextualized to meet local needs without losing alignment. Consistency in purpose doesn't mean uniformity in execution."

Shawn emphasized, "This allows your Identity to anchor all messaging while respecting each team's unique context."

## Strategic Environments: Defining Where Communication Takes Place

Shawn moved to the second layer of the Hive Effect: Strategic Environments. "Now that we've discussed Organizational Identity– the 'why' behind everything you do–it's time to talk about the spaces where that mission is carried out. These are your Strategic Environments."

"Environments are the bridge between your mission's Identity and the people you're serving. They represent the 'what,' 'when,' 'where,' and 'how' of communication and action in your ministry. They're not just physical places–they're categories of engagement. They define the spaces where ministry happens and communication takes place."

Shawn continued, "For a hive to thrive, it relies on more than just the structure of the hive itself. Bees navigate and interact with an expansive ecosystem–fields for gathering nectar, forests providing protection, gardens supplying diverse sources of nourishment, and the hive itself. Together, these ecosystems create the Environments where their work is possible, sustaining both the hive and the surrounding community. In ministry, Strategic Environments function in the same way: they are the physical and relational spaces where your mission connects with people, from church services to volunteer gatherings to community outreach events."

Matt added, "This is the middle layer of the Hive Effect. At the top, you have your Identity, anchoring everything. At the bottom, you have Archetypes—the people you're serving. Environments are the connection point, the structure that gives communication a context. While Environments provide overarching categories for mission engagement, they allow for flexibility in how messaging and strategies adapt to different cultural and ministry contexts."

Shawn nodded. "Every ministry has Environments, whether you've defined them or not. For some, it might be weekend services, small groups, or podcasts. For others, it could be donor events, online courses, or orphanages. The key is to intentionally define these spaces so they guide both communication and action."

Emily raised her hand, curious. "So, how do Environments help us align communication?"

"Great question," Shawn responded. "Environments provide clarity. They ensure that every message—whether it's from leadership to volunteers, from one department to another, or from your ministry to the outside world—is tailored to fit the context of where it's being delivered. For example, the way you communicate with a parent attending a family ministry event is different from how you connect with someone exploring discipleship for the first time."

Matt stepped in. "And this is where Environments really shine. They create boundaries—not to restrict but to focus. Each Environment becomes a unique setting for ministry, helping your team deliver the right message, at the right time, in the right way."

Shawn followed up. "Environments also allow for feedback. They're dynamic spaces where communication flows both ways—from the top level of Identity down to the Archetypes, and from the Archetypes back up to Identity. This ensures that your mission remains clear, adaptable, and aligned with the real-world needs of those you serve."

The group was attentive, recognizing how defining Environment categories could bring much-needed clarity and alignment to their ministries.

Shawn concluded, "Strategic Environments aren't just physical spaces—*they're pathways for your mission*. They help you ask and answer the critical questions: Where is ministry happening? What's the purpose of this space? How does it connect to the people we're serving? And how do these Environments reinforce the mission in everything we do?"

"We'll explore how these Environments apply to each of your organizations in more detail later, but for now, let's turn our attention to the 'who,'" Matt said, guiding the discussion forward.

## Audience Segments (Archetypes): The "Who"

The next layer of the Hive Effect is audience segments, what we call *Archetypes*. Shawn explained, "Archetypes represent the various groups of people you serve. They're the 'who for' in your relationship strategy, helping you tailor messages to meet specific needs and journeys within your community."

He paused, looking around the room. "And here's where MissionHive takes a unique approach. Archetypes aren't just labels—they're a way to see your audience as individuals on distinct journeys. Each Archetype encapsulates a unique perspective or set of needs, allowing you to shape communication that resonates deeply."

"In the hive, worker bees take on roles based on the hive's current needs. Some venture into the fields to collect pollen and nectar, essential resources that sustain the colony. Others stay within the hive, caring for the larvae, constructing honeycombs, or guarding the entrance. These roles shift as the hive's needs evolve, ensuring the colony remains strong and cohesive. Similarly, Archetypes in your ministry represent the diverse groups of people engaging with your mission—whether they're recruiting new volunteers, nurturing growth through discipleship, or building structures to support the community. Just as the hive thrives when each bee contributes uniquely to the whole, your ministry flourishes when Archetypes are understood and supported in ways that meet their specific journeys and contributions to the mission. Each member of the community serves and is served by the whole community."

Matt added, "The important part of establishing Archetypes is creating categories that reflect the core segments of people connected to your organization. These aren't just internal categories; they're the foundation for understanding your audience universally, across every campus, region, or ministry."

Shawn emphasized, "And remember, each Archetype is on a journey. Individuals in these categories progress through stages of engagement and involvement, experiencing and responding to your mission differently as they grow. We'll explore these stages more fully soon, but for now, keep in mind that Archetypes allow you to approach communication with nuance—meeting people where they are in their journey."

Jeremy from HRCC nodded confidently. "So, understanding these Archetypes helps us connect better with each person at every stage."

"You got it," Matt said, "and recognizing these stages helps you align your communication to meet people where they are. Whether you're engaging a new volunteer, a donor, or a long-time disciple, knowing their stage lets you speak to their unique needs and motivations. As one executive I've heard put it, it helps us communicate with people as if we know them.

Shawn added, "The needs of someone exploring faith will differ from a parent navigating family ministry or a volunteer building community. Like worker bees that adapt to their environment, people may fit in multiple Archetypes simultaneously. A parent Archetype might also be a volunteer Archetype and a donor. By understanding these distinctions, you can create communication that resonates deeply, reinforcing your mission while empowering individuals to find their unique place and contribution in the larger community."

The staff exchanged looks, realizing how these Archetypes and stages could add depth to their communication efforts. From Shawn and Matt's perspective, this was very rewarding, as many times ministry leaders and volunteers know something needs to change, but they don't know where to begin. These first "aha" moments set the tone for the rest of the workshops.

## The Hive Effect in Action: From Top-Down to Bottom-Up Flow

"Now, let's talk about how the Hive Effect works in practice," Shawn continued. "Think of it as a flow that connects every level. It starts with the Identity, moves down to the Specific Environments, and finally reaches the Archetypes."

He paused, letting this sink in. "But it doesn't end there. It works as a two-way communication flow, empowering each Archetype's needs to move upward, ultimately refining the organization's Identity and approach to Environments. When this flow is functioning well, your organization operates as an interconnected, mission-driven system—what we call a beecosystem."

Emily quickly asked, "Does that mean feedback from our field volunteers can actually influence the central mission?"

"Yes, and it should," Matt answered, "but it's about listening with purpose. This isn't a free-for-all where anyone speaks into any topic at any time. That would be chaotic. But timely, relevant feedback from every level is crucial for mission alignment and improvement. When a field volunteer shares insights from their experience, it helps ensure the mission stays grounded in reality. This is how silos break down—not by controlling every message, but by listening and adapting where necessary."

 MISSION HIVE OS         **"BEECOSYSTEM"**

### What is a Beecosystem?

The beecosystem is the natural outcome of the Hive Effect in action. It's a dynamic, interconnected organization where every team member's contributions flow together to create unity and mission alignment. Like bees working in harmony to sustain their hive, a beecosystem thrives when communication flows purposefully in all directions. This ensures that both strategic decisions and field-level insights strengthen the mission without creating silos or chaos.

Pastor Greg spoke up: "And how does senior leadership's authority fit here?"

Shawn responded carefully and clearly, "The Hive Effect doesn't combat senior leadership. In fact, it supports it by aligning every level to the 'Why' rooted in your Identity. But it also requires that senior leadership respects insights from every level, adapting when something is outside the mission scope. This approach isn't about diminishing authority; it's about making leadership truly mission-centered."

Matt added, "With this alignment, everyone gains the power to say 'no' when something strays from mission alignment—respectfully, of course. If a task or project doesn't align, this framework allows everyone to raise that concern. That's the essence of empowerment."

As the day's session wrapped up, Shawn summarized the core of the Hive Effect. "It is about bringing everyone into alignment with a shared purpose amidst the real complexity of our work. It's not about control—it's about clarity, unity, and a two-way flow of understanding that empowers missional action from top to bottom and bottom to top."

### Aha Moment

For the first time, HRCC and FaithLink saw how the Hive Effect could bridge the gaps, transforming communication from a fragmented process to a collaborative flow that united every department, ministry, and region around a shared purpose.

### Reflect & Apply

Consider your own organization's communication flow: Where do bottlenecks or misalignments occur? Think about how the Hive Effect could help unify your message without sacrificing individual ministry or department creativity.

# CHAPTER NINE

# Archetypes: Defining Who You Serve

*"An institution is a fellowship of persons united by community of purpose. Mechanism is an assembly of parts linked by interrelatedness of function. Purpose belongs to persons, function to things. Function is enslavement to an automatic process governed from without. Purpose is the expression of the living personal will. It is scarcely necessary to say that the supreme Archetype of the living institution is the Church."*

**Harry Blamires**

The next morning, the team gathered once again in the training facility, their energy renewed despite many of the team not getting much sleep. Some shared that they had been lying in bed thinking about the Hive Effect and reflecting on their learning with renewed optimism. Several said that they had annoyed their spouses by talking about the day non-stop until bedtime.

Jeremy King was so excited that he spent several hours texting with Matt and Shawn late into the evening, externally processing and connecting the dots and riffing about how the second campus (and its 50 plus volunteers) could thrive in this new model.

Another senior staff member confided in Shawn that he had just about given up hope that things could change and was considering moving on. However, the last couple days renewed his vigor and determination to stay the course. "With MissionHive," he said, "the future looks exciting."

All this feedback showed that those who had come in as skeptics were starting to become believers.

Today's focus would be pivotal—defining the audiences each ministry served—a process that Matt and Shawn particularly loved. Shawn opened the session, standing in front of both groups before they broke off into separate spaces. "Yesterday, we introduced the concept of the Hive Effect in organizational communications. Because each of your ministries already has Identity statements that guide your missional efforts, we don't need to spend additional time defining this part of the Hive Effect. Instead, today we're honing in on your Archetypes–the core categories of people your ministries serve."

Matt stepped up next to him, adding, "The Archetypes give you clarity on who your audience is, making sure that each message and every decision is aligned with the real needs and perspectives of those you're here to serve. Like every bee knows and carries out a variety of roles in the beecosystem, so your ministries must know and connect with every member of your community for the mission to be achieved."

Matt continued, "There are two main types of Archetypes: research-based and assumption-based. We will focus on assumption-based Archetypes using your expertise because it is easier in this setting, but you can always feel free in the future to supplement or correct your assumptions with research you gather from surveys, conversations, or focus groups. Let's break into our separate rooms to work through this process step by step."

With that, the HRCC team followed Matt into a neighboring room, while Shawn remained with the FaithLink team. Both groups would be working through the same structured process, but each would generate unique Archetypes that reflected their distinct ministries.

## Workshop One: HRCC's Archetype Development with Matt

In the HRCC room, Matt approached a whiteboard, marker in hand, ready to dive into the day's work. "Alright, team," he began, "we're going to start by thinking deeply about all the types of people HRCC engages with. This isn't just about giving names to broad groups–it's about understanding the people you're here to serve through relationships by considering their needs, perspectives, and journeys. Ministry messaging is about self-disclosure not self-promotion. It reflects how God is working through your ministry's community to change lives. So, we must connect with people intentionally and personally."

He paused, scanning the room as team members exchanged curious glances. To help bring the concept to life, he pulled up a slide on a TV monitor showing DC Comics' Batman and Joker. He explained that "when we think of specific heroes and villains, like Batman and the Joker, we are actually seeing Persona level details. Harry Potter and Luke Skywalker are also both unique Personas, with their own stories, adventures, timelines and universes. For organizations, it is very difficult to build mission-driven strategies that connect with every unique Persona. Shawn and I believe ministries need to think one level higher."

On the next slide he highlighted that the term "Archetype" comes from literature. They are character types, story lines or events that are notably recurrent across the human experience (Brown, 2021). Matt shared, "Potter, Skywalker, and Batman are Personas that would fall under the *Hero* Archetype. The Joker, Voldemort, and Darth Vader would be categorized as *Villain* Archetypes. These broader categories create a sense of familiarity that is common in our unique experiences. In our ministry context, our Archetypes aren't based firmly in literary characters, but they still represent the recurrent types of relationships you have within your community. They help us see the core journeys people are on as they engage with HRCC. If we effectively communicate with the *Hero* or *Villain* Archetype, every person in that group will relate to our message because it fits their perspective, needs, desires–their whole journey."

John McCall nodded slowly. "So, these are like patterns of connection we have with people?"

"Exactly," Matt confirmed, excited and a little surprised to see John picking it up so fast. "Think of Archetypes as recognizing these patterns and building relational profiles to interact with them. For us in ministry, it's the story of how you create meaningful, mission-centered experiences with and for your community."

"Shawn constantly quotes Bernadette Jiwa who wrote that '*Marketing is not a department,*'" he added, "'*it's the story of how you create difference for your customers*' (Jiwa, 61). If we don't understand the people we serve and build community with, we cannot effectively connect with them. And this isn't the responsibility of just the Communications teams in ministry, everyone on staff must effectively understand how to make meaningful, relational connections.

Archetypes allow us to work from the same authentically relational, strategic playbook."

As the team absorbed this concept, you could see their perspective on Archetypes for HRCC visibly shifting. "We're leveling up!" Jeremy exclaimed, breaking the tension and prompting a wave of laughter around the room.

"Classic campus pastor." Matt added with a playful grin, prompting even more laughter.

## Clarifying Personas vs. Archetypes

Maya raised a question, "We've tried working with Personas before, but it's been difficult to manage them. They seem so specific that we'd need hundreds to cover everyone we serve. Are we going to have the same issue with Archetypes?"

"That's a common struggle," Matt acknowledged. "But think back to the *heroes* and *villains* illustration. Personas can be incredibly granular, which is helpful in some contexts, and honestly a lot of fun for many of us Communications professionals, but that can be challenging for a large ministry. You'd need dozens, even hundreds, to capture every individual type. Persona is short for *personification* of the Archetype. That's where we add in the granular details of individuals within an Archetype. Personas get very specific. In a broader sense, Archetypes bring clarity to a complex range of relationships. They simplify the strategic process, making it possible to communicate effectively without getting lost in too many details." Matt continued with a half grin, "And spoiler alert, once your Archetypes are in place and well understood, each ministry will have the latitude to create their own personas anytime they want to or need to. 5-8 Archetypes, though, can usually serve the entire organization's needs making them much easier to grasp and simpler to use than dozens or hundreds of Personas."

The room visibly relaxed and were dismissed for a 15-minute break before the hard work would begin.

## Brainstorming Relationship Types and Defining Categories

While the team was on a break, Matt dropped several packs of sticky notes and pens on each table. When everyone returned, Matt continued, "Let's start by brainstorming all the types of people HRCC engages with—be as specific as possible, even down to persona-type details. We're going to fill these walls with every type of person that comes to mind." He paused and repeated himself, "*every single person that comes to mind. Don't hold back!*"

The room buzzed with activity as everyone began jotting down ideas on sticky notes. Soon, the walls were filled with descriptors: regular attendees, occasional visitors, young families, singles, high school students, recent retirees, those seeking spiritual growth, and people in crisis who turned to the church for support. Some were even more granular, divorced mom with a special needs child, or homeless man who needs help getting an ID. Matt even saw one that just said, "democrats" which made him giggle a little bit. They were getting it.

Once the wall was covered, Michael spoke up, "This is a lot to take in. It almost feels chaotic."

Matt nodded, smiling. "It's supposed to feel a bit overwhelming right now. The diversity of people HRCC serves is immense, and maybe you are all seeing the full scope of your relationships for the first time. These sticky notes represent a lot of complexity that exists among your community. But this is where we start organizing and making things simpler."

After spending the past several days with the group and forging new relationships, Matt felt comfortable asking the room to take a leap of faith and to trust him, to which they agreed.

## Segmenting the Types: Geographic, Demographic, Psychographic, and Behavioral

"We'll now segment these types into common categories— *Geographic, Demographic, Psychographic*, and *Behavioral*. This will help us categorize these sticky notes into clearer, manageable Archetypes."

Matt led them through each category, explaining the distinctions. "Geographic factors could include where people are coming from—are they local, from neighboring towns, or attending online? Demographics include age, marital status, and family structure. Psychographic covers attitudes, beliefs, and values, while Behavioral focuses on interaction patterns—such as their frequency of attendance or ministry involvement."

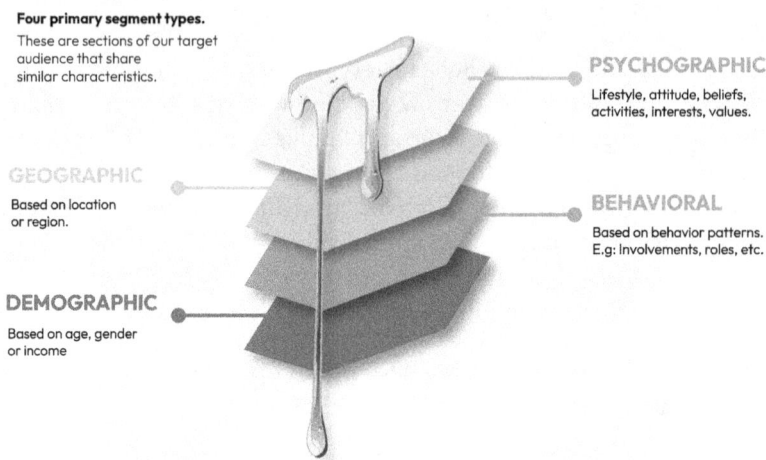

**Four primary segment types.**
These are sections of our target audience that share similar characteristics.

PSYCHOGRAPHIC
Lifestyle, attitude, beliefs, activities, interests, values.

GEOGRAPHIC
Based on location or region.

BEHAVIORAL
Based on behavior patterns. E.g: Involvements, roles, etc.

DEMOGRAPHIC
Based on age, gender or income

The team started sorting the sticky notes. They found that some groups, like "young families" and "single parents," fit well under Demographic. Others, like "those seeking growth" or "people in crisis," resonated more with Psychographic attributes. Behavioral types included categories like "frequent attendees," "holiday visitors," and "small group participants."

Pastor Greg looked over the segments, furrowing his brow. "I feel like some of these people fit in multiple categories. And we have a few that don't seem to fit anywhere."

"That's normal," Matt said. "Part of the process is noticing the patterns and the outliers. Sometimes, they reveal needs or perspectives that we may not have addressed fully or that we haven't fully "seen" in our day-to-day. It's also why this process is so valuable—it helps us ensure that everyone is seen and heard within your ministry." Matt explained it more directly, "This shows us that we aren't leaving anyone behind."

## Refining into Archetypes

After considerable discussion, the team condensed the various types into five core Archetypes and agreed on names for each one: *Seeker, Disciple, Volunteer, Neighbor in Need,* and *Parent.* They looked up at the final list on the board, a sense of clarity beginning to replace the initial chaos.

"This is really great work," Matt said encouragingly. "These Archetypes represent the core relationships you have with your community. They're your guide for aligning every message, decision, and action with the real needs of the people you're serving."

The entire group was feeling proud of the work they had done together.

"I want to pause here," Matt said, "because we are missing a critical segment. In fact, it is the most overlooked segment Shawn and I encounter in workshops like this."

"So close!" shouted Jeremy, raising his clenched fist in front of him.

Matt continued, laughing with the group. "No one wrote down "staff" on a post-it note. Isn't that interesting?"

"Wait. What? Seriously?" Jeremy said, indignant at the oversight.

Facetiously consoling Jeremy with a hand on his shoulder, Matt affirmed the group. "It's alright-this happens every time. For some reason, we stop seeing the critical and relational communication needed among one another as staff." Matt continued with a smile, "Well, at least you're not falling into the trap of thinking only about yourselves! You just affirmed the old saying–the shoemaker's kids always go barefoot."

"It's critical to prioritize how you communicate internally. If you're not considering each other and maintaining clear, mission-focused communication within your teams, how can you expect to stay aligned and mission-centric?"

With the room feeling equal parts satisfied and anxious, Matt shared an encouraging quote, "Another quote Shawn and I find helpful from Bernadette Jiwa is, 'We are at our very best when we see the world through the eyes of the person we're trying to matter to (Jiwa, 23).' These Archetypes help you do just that–see your ministry through the eyes of the people it's meant for."

As the quote set in, the room started clapping and high-fiving as their accomplishment started to come into full view. Pastor Greg sat in the back grinning from ear to ear as he saw that, for the first time in a long time, everyone's fears and anxieties were starting to be replaced with optimism and excitement. "This is cool, he thought. Really cool."

## Building the Archetype Profile: Mapping the Journey with Empathy

After another short break Matt quieted the room and began, turning to the next part of the workshop, "we're going to take one Archetype and build out a six-stage journey profile." He introduced the six stages that each Archetype progresses through on their journey: *Lack of Awareness, Awareness, Consideration, Involvement, Support & Service,* and *Loyalty & Advocacy.*

Matt continued, "In the top-level section of each journey stage, we'll use a tool called Empathy Mapping to help us understand the Archetype from their perspective. He pulled up a slide on the TV monitor showing an "X" with a single word or short sentence in each quadrant. This map has four sections: *Think & Feel, Hear, Say & Do,* and *See.* It allows us to put ourselves in their mindset, to consider what they're experiencing and feeling at each stage."

They selected the "Seeker" as their starting Archetype and began mapping its journey. In the first stage, they explored what a "Seeker" might be thinking and feeling when they first encounter HRCC. Team members suggested that these individuals might feel uncertain but hopeful, looking for a sense of belonging or purpose.

Kim, raised her hand. "How do we incorporate the doubts or hesitations they might have? Should we focus only on the positives?"

"Good question," Matt replied. "Empathy Mapping is about stepping fully into their shoes. We want to acknowledge their doubts and challenges as well as their hopes. A Seeker might feel skeptical yet curious. Capturing this helps us connect authentically."

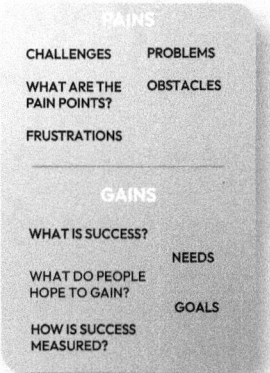

As Matt was walking around the room sneaking glances at their notebooks, he interrupted with a word of advice from his experiences doing these workshops with other organizations.

"With these empathy maps, you need to take the prompt literally. So for instance, *what they see* should be things that they are seeing with their eyes." Matt continued, "it could be graphics, signage, smiling volunteers in the parking lot, gum in the carpet, broken links in email newsletters."

"Frequently in ministry Environments, we want to take things deeper and more ethereal, and people will say things like "they are seeing life change." That's cool, but what we are looking for is what they are seeing with their eyeballs. To fully understand the audience we need to know what they are actually seeing and feeling in the context of Harvest Ridge."

A few people giggled as they crossed off a few items on their lists.

As they worked through each stage of the Seeker Archetype, Matt guided them to fill out the journey map. For each stage, they discussed the Seeker's point-of-view (using their Empathy Mapping insights), their obstacles, HRCC's response, the Seeker's response, and Environmental touchpoints—a point where the mission touches someone's life in a deep way, both digital and in-person—that would allow meaningful interaction. This brought depth to their understanding, helping them see how HRCC could meet the Seeker's needs across different points in their journey.

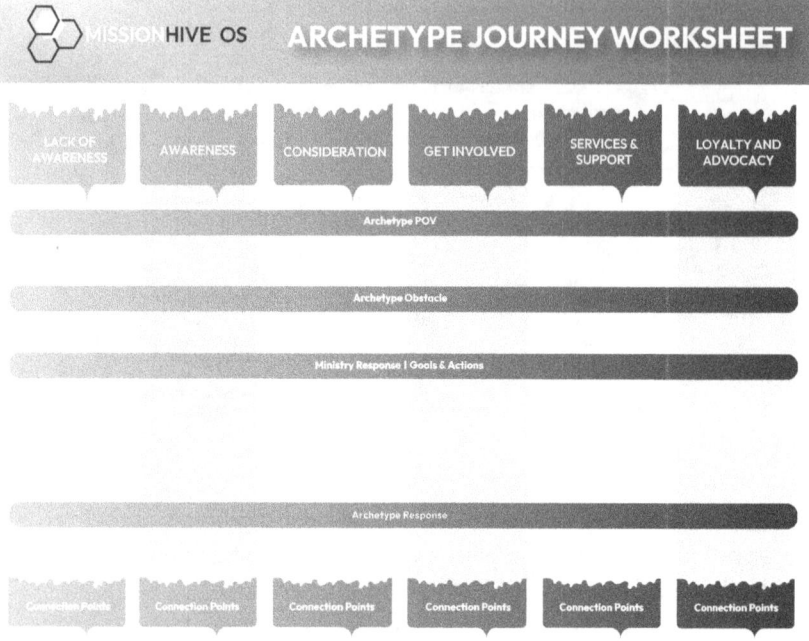

At the final stage, after completing the map, the room was filled with a sense of accomplishment. Pastor Greg looked at the chart and said, "This isn't just a map; it's a framework for truly walking alongside people."

Matt nodded. "That's exactly the purpose of Archetypes in MHOS—to create genuine connection and alignment with the people you serve. This is a *ready-aim-fire strategy*, instead of ready-fire-aim *tactics*."

Greg's revelation and Matt's response had clearly sparked something deeper. Jeremy, usually the lighthearted one in the room, suddenly turned serious. "Wow," he said. "Jesus modeled Archetypes and journeys perfectly. Maybe by leaning into this process, we're actually becoming more Christlike."

The room fell silent for a moment, the weight of Jeremy's insight sinking in. Heads nodded as people exchanged glances, each person visibly struck by his realization.

Sensing the moment, Matt added, "Think about Peter's life in the Bible—it's a tremendous Archetype journey. He literally moves from a *Seeker* to a *Disciple*, and then through the gospels, Acts, and his own writings, we see him move across all the discipleship stages from lack of awareness to becoming a foundational advocate of the Great Commission. His story shows us what transformation can look like when it's guided by clarity, care, and purpose."

Matt affirmed the progress HRCC staff were making on their Archetype journeys, and encouraged them to keep developing each one. Staff were invigorated by this process, feeling like they were *truly* seeing their community through a whole new lens.

## Workshop Two: FaithLink's Archetype Development with Shawn

In the neighboring room, Shawn gathered with the FaithLink team, guiding them through the same foundational steps Matt had introduced to HRCC but adapted to address FaithLink's specific challenges and international scope. The sticky notes exercise was wrapping up, with team members filling the wall with characteristics and descriptions of the various groups they served globally.

Shawn said, "For FaithLink, Archetypes give us a structured way to simplify complexity across your global regions and allow for unified messaging without losing local relevance. Unlike Personas, which often end up being too narrow and hard to manage, Archetypes bring focus and clarity, allowing FaithLink to stay mission-centered even across different cultural contexts."

Nods around the room confirmed understanding, and several team members began peeling back layers on FaithLink's unique audience. Maya took the opportunity to voice a common challenge. "Sometimes, we feel like we're caught between the need to localize our messaging and the need to maintain a consistent voice across regions. Can Archetypes really help us achieve both?"

Shawn nodded, "Absolutely. That's the power of Archetypes in a mission-centered framework. They even help you bridge cultural and contextual differences by focusing on universal needs and motivations that exist in all people—while allowing room for nuance in the actual messaging. Each Archetype provides an anchor point, ensuring that all messaging aligns with FaithLink's mission, regardless of different nuances that shape your interactions."

Over the next couple of hours, Shawn guided the FaithLink team through the same dynamic exercise of segmentation and Archetype naming like Matt had facilitated with HRCC–also ensuring "staff" was added to their list. By the end, FaithLink had reached a consensus on their Archetypes, identifying six key groups that define their mission: *General Donors, Major Donors, National Partner Organizations, Staff, Field Volunteers,* and *Students*. Each Archetype reflected a distinct and vital part of their ministry, offering a clear lens through which to understand and engage their diverse community.

## Stages of the Archetype Journey

Shawn encouraged the team to begin mapping out one of their most crucial Archetypes mentioned numerous times in the first days of the workshops: the General Donor. He also introduced the six stages that each Archetype progresses through on their journey, from initial *Lack of Awareness* to *Advocacy & Loyalty*.

"Let's walk through each stage of the journey for this Archetype," Shawn said. "We'll use empathy mapping to understand the General Donor's point of view in each stage, and then discuss how FaithLink can engage, serve, and support them effectively."

Starting with *Lack of Awareness*, Shawn prompted, "Think about someone who doesn't yet know FaithLink exists. What do you imagine they think and feel? What are they hearing, seeing, saying, or doing?"

The team filled in responses, drawing on empathy to inhabit the Donor's perspective. In this early stage, the group imagined the Donor feeling a general desire to make a difference but lacking direction or awareness of FaithLink. "They might be hearing about poverty or global issues through the media, but they haven't connected those concerns to an organization like ours," David offered.

Maya added, "And their pain points might be around wanting to help but not knowing where to start."

Shawn nodded, guiding them to think through FaithLink's ministry response. "In this stage, your goal isn't to ask for commitment but to create an opening–raise awareness and invite curiosity. You'll find Environments and channels to connect with them relationally."

At the next stage, *Awareness*, the team imagined the General Donor starting to recognize FaithLink's presence, perhaps through social media or a friend's recommendation. FaithLink's action at this stage, they determined, would involve gentle, informative introductions that link the Donor's general desire for impact with FaithLink's mission. Touchpoints could include digital content, educational videos, and thought-provoking campaigns.

"Now, let's move to *Consideration*," Shawn continued. "At this point, they know about you, but they're weighing their options. How do we engage them meaningfully here?"

James suggested, "We could emphasize stories from the field—showing the tangible impact of their potential support."

"That's exactly right," Shawn responded. "Your role here is to establish credibility. Through stories, testimonials, and open communication, you help the Donor see that supporting FaithLink will be a trusted, impactful choice."

As they advanced to *Involvement*, the team recognized this as the stage where the Donor takes their first action. "At this point, we need to create easy, accessible avenues for them to get involved—whether it's a one-time donation, a volunteer opportunity, or attending a local event," said Maya. Shawn affirmed this insight, noting that touchpoints here should make involvement seamless and rewarding.

At *Support & Service*, Shawn noted that most ministries tend to abandon a person at the fourth stage of their journey, and this is a big mistake. He explained, "If we stop engaging them once they accept our call-to-action, at *Involvement*, we start treating them in a utilitarian, transactional way. We must never do this, or we come across as dismissive. Instead, we must continue to invest in the relationship as personally as we can—treating them as equal partners in the mission who are enabling transformation. For donors specifically, giving is an act of worship. We must acknowledge and respect that."

Shawn then had the team consider how FaithLink could maintain engagement and deepen the relationship. "They're now supporting the mission," he noted. "What do they need and want to remain connected to it?"

The team brainstormed touchpoints that would communicate appreciation and demonstrate ongoing impact—such as periodic newsletters, personalized updates, and invitations to special events. "In this stage, FaithLink would start to become a consistent part of the Donor's life, not just a cause they give to," David suggested.

Finally, they reached *Loyalty & Advocacy*, the stage where the General Donor becomes a champion for FaithLink, actively sharing its mission with others. Here, FaithLink's role was to empower these Advocates, giving them resources and opportunities to spread the word.

"This final stage is crucial," Shawn emphasized. "The relationship doesn't end here—it grows. You'll want to provide tools, stories, and ways for them to feel like an integral part of FaithLink's work. Equip them to be an ambassador of the mission, both educating them more deeply and helping them educate others."

"This is where the flywheel concept comes into the picture. He paused for a moment before explaining the process, "picture a cyclist pedaling along a bike trail. At first, every push of the pedals feels like it takes all their strength to move the bike forward. But as the wheels gain speed, the flywheel—a small, powerful mechanism—kicks in. It stores the energy from the rider's effort, creating a steady momentum that carries the cyclist forward, even during moments when their legs pause or ease off. The ride becomes smoother, requiring less effort to maintain speed, and the cyclist can focus more on enjoying the journey rather than constantly pushing against inertia."

"In much the same way, the Loyalty & Advocacy phase in your Archetype journeys works like the flywheel. Early in someone's journey, the ministry invests significant effort to build trust, provide value, and connect them to the mission. But as they progress, the relationship develops momentum. Loyal Advocates, like the cyclist benefiting from the flywheel, continue to move the mission forward with less direct effort from the ministry's staff. They become energized partners, sustaining and amplifying the work through their passion, resources, and voices. This phase isn't about easing off altogether—it's about leveraging the energy stored in their experiences and commitment, creating a sustainable rhythm that advances the mission with joyful collaboration. This is how true multiplication happens in ministry—and is exactly how Jesus equipped His disciples to build and sustain His global Church."

Emily, exhaling peacefully, commented, "Isn't it wild how simple things really can be and how much Jesus modeled how to do ministry? We make things so hard sometimes. Thank you for bringing us back to basics in a way that seems so manageable and so relational. I needed this." Her team nodded in agreement.

Shawn wrapped up with the FaithLink team, encouraging them to continue working on the rest of the Archetype journeys. Like the HRCC team, the staff were energized by what they had created together in such a short time. More work remained ahead, but the team was now prepared to keep building these tools for their toolbox.

## Debriefing Together

At the end of the intensive day, the HRCC and FaithLink teams reconvened together, the room buzzing with insights from their deep dives into Archetypes. Shawn and Matt stood at the front, ready to guide the debrief, bridging Archetypes with the broader Hive Effect introduced the day before.

Shawn opened with encouragement. "It sounds like you've had some powerful realizations. Let's hear those 'aha moments' from today."

Maya spoke first. "I realized that Archetypes aren't just static Personas—they offer dynamic depth and flexibility. They let us meet people where they are without losing sight of our core mission."

James added, "For me, it was seeing how Archetypes can work universally across regions without sacrificing cultural relevance or diluting our mission focus."

Matt affirmed their reflections. "Exactly. Archetypes anchor your messaging in mission-driven categories, adaptable across contexts but always rooted in purpose."

John from HRCC shared another key insight. "We saw how much we've been missing by treating everyone as if they're in the same stage of engagement. Recognizing the six stages of Archetype journeys helped us see where our communication has fallen short."

Jeremy added, "It's like we've been speaking to everyone the same way and wondering why it didn't always connect. Now we can fix that. And the *flywheel* of Advocacy was huge for me."

Matt nodded. "This is where the Hive Effect ties it all together. Aligned communication—across Identity, Environments, and Archetypes—reinforces your mission and prevents silos. Misalignment creates breakdowns, but the Hive Effect keeps everything connected. And the flywheel joins everyone together meaningfully to share the load and live out our missional work."

Michael raised a tension he was feeling. "For us at Harvest Ridge, one of the challenges has been maintaining a cohesive mission without controlling every detail. I don't want to micromanage, but I also don't want things to veer off track."

Matt nodded, recognizing the familiar tension. "That's the beauty of the Hive Effect—it's not about top-down control; it's about embedding the mission in each layer to move the mission forward in ways that feel natural and authentic. When your teams are equipped with this kind of healthy alignment, they have the clarity and autonomy to communicate without constant intervention from leadership. It's about setting up a framework that's flexible, but focused."

Shawn added, "And, again, this framework also gives your teams the confidence to say 'no' to ideas or tasks that stray from your mission. When your culture operates this way, it actually frees up time to focus on what matters because you are not breaking and repairing things all the time. It's not just about giving permission, but offers an invitation for everyone to guard the mission actively. You're empowering staff and key volunteers to protect the organization's purpose, while keeping your Archetypes in focus."

The room grew quiet, the weight of shared responsibility settling in. Michael broke the silence. "So, it's less about compliance and more about contribution?"

Shawn smiled. "Exactly. It's a dynamic flow—top-down and bottom-up. Insights, concerns, and ideas travel through the organization far more efficiently and effectively than top-down directives. That's how you build trust and engagement."

James added, "This sounds like a way to eliminate bottlenecks and keep everyone invested in the outcome. That's good stewardship."

Pastor Greg voiced the closing thought on everyone's minds. "If we implement this system, I think we'll finally have the clarity and

trust we've been missing. I can see our teams being empowered–
not because they're following orders, but because they're deeply
connected to the mission."

He then paused, becoming visibly emotional as tears welled up in his
eyes, and the room filled with interest. "All I've ever wanted since we
planted Harvest Ridge 20-years ago was to have a group of people
mobilized for the mission *with me*, not *for me*. Yes, we're growing–
but I have not been at peace with the way things are. Today I am
beginning to see clearly where we have gone wrong, and I see that
MissionHive offers really good solutions."

"Thank you for sharing, Greg. It has been a joy to watch each of you
process this week." Shawn concluded, "And we aren't done yet.
Tomorrow, we'll explore strategic Environments and how they connect
your mission to the people you serve."

They closed out the day with a time of prayer and left for home, tired
from the work but excited for what tomorrow would bring.

### Aha Moment

The teams discovered that Archetypes are not merely static
categories or marketing tools; they are dynamic relational profiles
that help ministries connect deeply and authentically with their
communities. By recognizing the six stages of engagement for
each Archetype, they saw the critical importance of tailoring
communication to meet people where they are on their journey.
This clarity revealed how alignment across Identity, Environments,
and Archetypes fosters meaningful engagement, breaks down
silos, and keeps the mission at the forefront.

### Reflect & Apply

Reflect on the diversity of your ministry's audience. Are you
tailoring communication to meet people at different stages
of their journey, or are you treating everyone as if they are in
the same place? Identify one potential Archetype within your
organization and consider their unique needs, challenges, and
motivations. How might refining your approach to this Archetype
improve their connection to your mission and deepen their
engagement?

# CHAPTER TEN

# Strategic Environments: Where Communication Comes to Life

*"Ministry takes place when divine resources meet human needs through loving channels to the glory of God."*

**Warren Wiersbe**

The fourth morning of the workshops began with anticipation as representatives from both organizations gathered together once more. After three intense days of exploring the Hive Effect and refining their Archetypes, the teams from HRCC and FaithLink were visibly eager to tackle the final element of MHOS: *Strategic Environments*.

As everyone settled in their seats, Shawn introduced the day's focus. "Today, we're moving into the middle of the Hive Effect—Strategic Environments. If Identity grounds the *'why'* of your organization and Archetypes clarify *'who'* you serve, then Environments define the practical *'what, where, when,* and *how'* your mission comes to life. The mission tangibly engages people on the mission in Environments."

Matt jumped in to expand, "And just as each ministry is unique, these Environments won't be one-size-fits-all. What HRCC needs will be different from what FaithLink needs. But across both, the goal is to create adaptable, context-driven spaces that reflect your organization's mission. We're doing this session together as one group because we think you'll all benefit from hearing each other process your unique Environments. Comparing and contrasting is helpful in a process like this."

Matt directed the group to consider the various types of engagement that already existed within their organizations, urging them to think of the places where they connect most meaningfully with people day-to-day. He explained that limiting the Environments to three or four categories would be essential to keep them focused and effective. "Think of these as intentional spaces, each one designed to capture a distinct aspect of your mission," he continued.

The room was quiet as the participants were deeply focused. They understood that this step was pivotal, not just as another "piece" of MissionHive but the bridge that would link the foundational purpose of Identity and the personalized journeys of Archetypes.

"Let's approach this as a discovery process," Matt said, smiling. "We're not looking to fill in blanks. Instead, we'll refine and assess together until each Environment feels essential to your ministry."

## HRCC's Exploration of Environments

Pastor Greg broke the silence. "Well, we definitely know our Sunday gatherings are key. That's where we connect with most of our congregation."

"Absolutely," Shawn nodded. "Now, let's go beyond labels and dive into the essence. What happens there that's unique to Sunday gatherings?"

Greg considered this. "It's a place where people worship together, hear the Word, and often have their first interaction with our church. It's our largest touchpoint."

John added, "And then there's the fellowship—a true sense of belonging. It's more than just a service; it's a place where people feel deeply connected. And, of course, as the communications guy, I know it's also an invaluable Environment for sharing key messages with everyone simultaneously."

Shawn noted this on a whiteboard. "What you're describing is a relational space—a place of connection and fellowship, where people can find community as they engage in worship as well as being a place to strategically inform the group."

The team nodded, recognizing this as central. However, Jeremy brought up their digital services. "We've also been exploring our online reach. I wonder if online services should be an Environment in itself?"

Matt thought about it for a minute. "That's a fair point, Jeremy, but would you say the goal is similar to in-person gatherings? Or is online more of an extension—a digital expression of that relational space?"

Jeremy hesitated. "I suppose it's an extension. The goal is still about connecting people to worship and teaching, so maybe it doesn't need to stand alone."

This refinement allowed HRCC to focus on *Gatherings* as the Environment encapsulating all worship gatherings, in person and online, as spaces for connection and fellowship.

Moving forward, the team explored small groups, which Greg suggested as another core Environment. "We see real transformation there. It's intimate, and people grow spiritually. As the church has grown I'm not able to personally disciple everyone, so the small groups have become vital in that respect."

"Is the focus here more about personal connection or spiritual growth?" Matt asked, encouraging the group to clarify.

"Spiritual growth and community," John answered. "It's about depth. People come away with something personal, they take the messages from Sundays and look inward, practically applying the lessons to their lives and families all while building real community in a smaller setting."

"Then it sounds like we're talking about something transformational," Shawn observed. "A space dedicated to faith formation, community, and personal growth." He surveyed the room and saw each head nodding in approval. The team settled on *Life Community* to represent the small group Environment.

As they continued, HRCC briefly considered an Environment dedicated to internal training or leadership development, but ultimately, they agreed it didn't uniquely serve the mission in a standalone way but fit within the Gatherings and Life Community Environments. Instead, they focused on community outreach.

Jeremy spoke passionately about their commitment to the wider community. "We believe in getting outside the church walls. Serving people in need and sharing Christ's love beyond Sunday gatherings." He continued, "Thinking broadly, this is everything we do locally within our community to short-term missions trips and even our support of global missionaries and organizations, like FaithLink."

With agreement from the team, they defined Commissional as an Environment focused on external engagement, distinct from the internal, relational spaces of the church.

## FaithLink's Journey to Define Environments

Turning to FaithLink, Shawn encouraged them to follow HRCC's example. "Like Matt said earlier, think of this as a discovery process. Which spaces allow you to accomplish your mission?"

Emily spoke up. "FaithLink is focused heavily on relationship development in everything we do. Our engagement with donors and volunteers stands out. Without them, we can't operate."

"So would you say this Environment is about connection or empowerment?" Shawn asked.

"Connection," Emily replied. "It's how we bring them in and communicate why they matter."

After some discussion, they agreed on *Supporter Engagement* as a fitting name, noting that this is a relational Environment focused on building and nurturing relationships with general and major donors.

Maya suggested field support as a possible Environment. "Our field staff need resources to do their work. It's more than logistics; it's how we enable them to be effective."

James pointed out that "support" might not fully capture the empowerment they aimed to provide. "Our goal is more than providing resources. We're empowering our staff to serve with significant impact."

After some more back and forth, they settled on *Staff Empowerment* as a distinct Environment focused on equipping field teams with autonomy and resources.

They then turned to the primary purpose of FaithLink's work—its direct ministry to communities around the world.

James spoke with passion. "Our mission is to live out the Great Commission. We exist to serve communities in tangible ways that demonstrate God's love and meet their most pressing needs."

With consensus from the team, they named this Environment *Community Mission* to capture the heart of FaithLink's ministry efforts, directed toward living out the gospel and impacting lives within the communities they serve.

Now in a bit of a groove after locking in the others, FaithLink quickly identified *Partner Collaboration* as a fourth Environment, focused on fostering relationships with other organizations. These partnerships enabled FaithLink to provide holistic care to communities, collaborating on services and resources that FaithLink couldn't fulfill alone, but that were needed by the communities.

## Connecting Environments with the Hive Effect

With both teams having defined their Environments, Matt and Shawn guided them to understand how each Environment fit into the Hive Effect.

"Each of these Environments is now a context for your Archetypes and your ministry to connect," Matt explained. "You're creating spaces for every audience within your mission, guiding them through each stage of relationship."

Shawn added, "This movement isn't a static flow. Each Environment supports specific goals within your mission. When these layers align, you create a cohesive approach that empowers both your staff and your audience. Like all the Environments that are essential for a beehive to thrive, both inside and outside the hive, everything must contribute to your beecosystem."

Michael reflected on how this framework was changing his perspective. "Seems like we've often grouped communication around tasks, now I'm seeing how each Environment could guide our mission focus as we strategically pair our efforts with the Archetypes."

James agreed. "Seeing these categories now, I can envision how each message, each story we share, belongs to a specific Environment with its own audience."

Shawn took a moment to reinforce an essential point. "Keep in mind, MHOS isn't simply a communications system. While communication is a foundational component, MissionHive ultimately reshapes all areas of ministry—including support roles like creative, fundraising, and administrative functions. This affects everyone's work, aligning actions with mission in a way that brings the whole organization together. Every role is critical to the ministry."

He continued, "Imagine how this would transform your meetings. When each department has a clear Environment to focus on, discussions shift from isolated tasks to mission-centered conversations. In this approach, empowerment flows up and down the organization, guiding decisions while allowing every level to share ownership. Every activity meets your community where they are."

As the session started winding down, both teams had a clearer vision of how their newly defined Environments would begin to anchor their actions, engaging every Archetype while reinforcing the mission at all levels.

## Debrief: The Journey So Far and an Unexpected Realization

Before the session wrapped up, Matt and Shawn led the teams in a final debrief. Shawn, sensing the weight of the journey so far, broke the silence with a warm smile. "So, let's hear it—how are you all feeling about this process?"

There were nods and thoughtful murmurs. Maya spoke up first. "It's… a lot to take in. I can see the clarity that's forming, but honestly, implementing this for our whole organization feels daunting. This work feels like lifting a mountain, especially without you both here every day to guide us. To be honest, I'm a little nervous because we've tried to make changes in the past but over time they just didn't stick."

Greg added, "There's a real excitement, but I think we also feel the challenge of taking full ownership of something this comprehensive. We've relied on your guidance in every step this week, and the thought of doing this on our own is a bit intimidating. I don't want the joy and excitement I feel right now to fade when day-to-day pressures dial up. But I'm committed to this."

Shawn nodded, acknowledging their concerns. "I want you to know that we hear you. And we actually have a plan to help with that transition. You won't be left without support. We'll prepare you with tools to make sure MHOS becomes second nature for each of you, and we'll guide you through the initial steps as you take full ownership."

He then turned to Greg and Emily, and continued, "Making organizational changes stick is always challenging, and we get that. But remember, Matt and I are here to guide and support —you and your teams are the ones doing the real, transformative work. This is the beginning of a culture shift, not just a shift in process."

There was a collective exhale of relief around the room. Everyone looked visibly reassured and exchanged hopeful glances. As they were refocusing up front, Matt had one last thing he was excited to bring to the group.

"Ok," he said, "there's something else we want to reveal. You may not realize it, but we've been taking you through a journey of your own as a group. Each of you has already been on a six-stage journey…one that's directly tied to the structure you'll be using with your Archetypes."

Kim cracked a grin. "Wait, are you talking about an Archetype journey?"

"Yep," Matt replied. "Shawn and I have been guiding you through each stage, not just to introduce MHOS but to give you firsthand experience of how these journeys move people through the stages naturally. We have been showing you as well as teaching you."

Shawn joined in, "We began by establishing awareness. Then we moved you to consideration as you started seeing how MHOS could answer your challenges. Involvement came as you started engaging in workshops, trying out the system. Right now, you're moving into the support and service stage—equipping yourselves to implement MHOS with your teams. And you know the ultimate goal?

Jeremy interrupted, "Help you guys sell more books!" The room erupted in laughter.

"That would be great," Shawn said jokingly, but no." He paused as everyone settled back in, "The ultimate goal is loyalty and advocacy, but not to Matt and me. Soon, you'll not only understand MHOS but you'll advocate for it, bringing others in your organizations along the same journey you've experienced here."

The group, still smiling from Jeremy's interjection, shared a few nods and high fives as this reality sunk in.

As the room was quieting back down and in his usual near perfect timing, Pastor Greg shared, "It's like seeing the blueprint come to life in real-time. The six stages felt subtle, but looking back…I can see how each one has prepared us for this."

Maya nodded in agreement, her eyes bright with newfound understanding. "The process has felt natural, like we've been guided step-by-step. But now I see that wasn't an accident. It's actually a profound structure."

Matt smiled, letting their realizations deepen. "Exactly. MissionHive isn't just theory—it's a framework that, when practiced, becomes an intuitive way of moving people into mission alignment. You've lived it yourselves, and now, you can replicate it for the people you serve and serve with."

Shawn added, "And this is what makes MHOS different from other systems. It doesn't depend on us to function. You've built this process yourselves, certainly with our guidance, but it's something you'll be able to carry forward with less stress than you think."

As the significance of the week's accomplishments settled over the room, the teams were giddy, reflecting on their own journeys and the insights they'd gained along the way. They now saw MHOS not just as a set of guidelines but as a transformative experience they could share.

### Aha Moment

For the first time, HRCC and FaithLink realized the true depth of MHOS—not just as a framework but as a lived experience. They saw how the Environments element of the Hive Effect provides them with a roadmap for growth, alignment, and empowerment that could transform their ministries from the inside out.

### Reflect & Apply

Reflect on how your team currently approaches engagement, specifically in your Environments. Consider how the six stages of *Lack of Awareness, Awareness, Consideration, Involvement, Service & Support, Loyalty & Advocacy* might help you bring others on a collaborative journey. What would shift if your approach allowed each person to become an advocate for your mission everywhere that ministry happens?

# Part 5: Building a Culture of Alignment

## Hive Insight

This part delves into how MHOS fosters a transformative, organization-wide culture shift, grounded in shared values, mission clarity, and collaborative ownership. By focusing on alignment rather than control, MHOS empowers each leader, team, and individual to function as an integrated part of the ministry, reinforcing the mission through daily actions and strategic decisions. Readers will see how these shifts nurture both internal and external relationships, ensuring that every role supports a unified and mission-driven culture.

We will see Matt and Shawn prepare Greg, Emily, Maya, and John to lead the culture of alignment within their own organizations, building confidence to carry MHOS forward independently. These chapters explore how mission-first thinking clarifies the organization's Identity, strengthens cross-departmental collaboration, and empowers communications as a strategic component of ministry leadership, ensuring MissionHive becomes a sustainable system within each ministry.

# CHAPTER ELEVEN

# Identity-Driven Culture

*"A church's culture is its message.*
*Your culture is more powerful than your words."*

**Sam Chand**

The training facility felt different the next morning. With most of the HRCC and FaithLink staff having left, only four people remained with Matt and Shawn as they were set to dig into the senior-level operational aspects of MHOS: Pastor Greg Johnson and Communications Director John McCall from Harvest Ridge Community Church, along with Executive Director Emily Roberts and Communications Director Maya Gonzalez from FaithLink. This smaller group from each organization, created an intimate, almost contemplative atmosphere as they settled into the same meeting room where, just the day before, both teams had reached a new level of understanding about MHOS and had celebrated some big wins.

"Thank you all for staying another day," Shawn began. "Now comes the work of embedding MissionHive deeply into your culture to align your organizations with your mission and values."

Matt continued, "We're not talking about just a few tweaks to improve communication or adjust tactics; we're talking about creating a culture that is fully aligned with the mission and values that drive you. As you know, this is a primary function of senior leadership."

Emily nodded, visibly energized by the challenge. "Our teams are ready. The clarity we've gained feels transformational."

Greg agreed. "Now we need to make sure these concepts shape our daily operations. I'm excited for your insights on this part."

## Positioning Communications for Strategic Influence

Shawn addressed Greg and Emily directly. "We see the two of you as the primary advocates for MHOS and John and Maya as essential, uniquely qualified leaders to aid you. Matt and I believe that for MissionHive to be taught and adopted in every organization, the Communications director, whatever their title might be, must be a part of the senior leadership team. Their expertise and experience helps ensure MHOS doesn't just exist on paper but becomes the heartbeat of your organizations. This isn't about overhauling your organizational structure. It's about ensuring that MHOS has the voice and influence it needs to succeed."

Maya exchanged a glance with John, both of them sensing the significance of the moment. "For years, I've felt like our team's insights get lost in the noise of daily operations," John voiced. "Implementing MissionHive feels exciting, but also a bit daunting."

Matt addressed their insecurity. "I know that for both of you, stepping into this level of influence might feel overwhelming. Communications shapes the alignment of your mission. It's not merely support; it's a foundational strategy."

Greg and Emily listened intently, each reflecting on how this shift would play out in their organizations. Greg, ever focused on unity, raised a question. "How do we avoid creating any tension here? I don't want ministry leaders feeling like Communications is taking over their work or directing them. I want to make sure we stay collaborative."

Shawn spoke thoughtfully to the group. "I understand that empowering communications can feel like a shift from traditional ministry roles, and I've personally encountered these tensions."

He glanced at Matt, who nodded, then continued. "Years ago a regional leader urged me to take a global role because he perceived I was not staying in my lane. He saw my position as one that should be narrowly focused on tactical marketing or donor engagement, not one with a role in shaping the organization's ministry strategy."

Maya and John exchanged glances, clearly resonating with Shawn's story.

"A few months later, I took on a global operations role, and it was shortly after that some of the leaders in my former region began to understand the strategic insights I had been advocating for," Shawn said. "That experience partly shaped my philosophy for MHOS.

Communications roles shouldn't be sidelined; they are integral to the mission. It isn't merely a ministry support function-it is unequivocally proper ministry."

Greg understood, "I see what you mean. There are times when our Communications team's insights feel undervalued or have been ignored outright, but they've often pointed out things we've missed."

That resonates," said Emily. "I've seen how sidelining certain voices can cost us alignment in the long run. I know that Maya has immensely valuable perspective and intuition well beyond messaging. I'm sure Greg would say the same about John."

Maya was feeling energized. "So, if we're advocating for a more strategic communications role in leadership, it's not just about visibility. It's about placing all communications efforts, not just a team, as a cornerstone of our operational structure."

"Exactly," Matt affirmed. "Both of you, Maya and John, and your teams have critical insight into the organizational pulse because of your roles. You see patterns, disconnects, and opportunities in ways that are unique. Your perspective is essential–not tangential–to effective ministry."

To drive the point home, Matt shared an experience from his own career. "When I took on the communications director role at a large multi-site church, it felt like I was an air traffic controller, constantly coordinating to keep all the projects from colliding. A Communications team is like the organizational nuclear reactor. Every ministry relies on it, even if Communications doesn't oversee everyone else's work directly." He concluded, "What I learned is that communications teams are often an untapped source of invaluable insight–seeing both the big picture and the details that can make or break alignment."

Greg looked contemplative. "So, if Communications roles aren't just support but a cornerstone of MissionHive, we'd need to be clear on how we balance influence. Maya and John have insight, but we don't want to set up divisions or barriers between departments."

Shawn nodded, appreciating Greg's careful thought. "That's right–this isn't about dividing influence but about alignment and inclusion. Communications, operations, ministry, outreach, accounting, facilities– all parts of the organization serve the same mission. This is why we use the illustration of a hive in our framework. If Communications leaders like Maya and John are fully integrated with a voice and input at the senior level, it empowers the entire ministry to be aligned, with each team understanding its role in communicating the mission."

Emily, intrigued, asked, "How do we ensure ministry leaders see Communications staff as partners and not their directors? I want to avoid any sense of overreach."

Matt took this one. "Practically, this means that John and Maya would be included in strategic conversations alongside other senior leaders, with an equal voice. They're not serving as internal consultants or "sometimes" strategists; they're essential, equal leaders in the entire mission. Their voice, expertise, and guidance are vital for your mission to succeed. Communications doesn't control; it connects. This adjustment helps unify the mission, not position one team to compete for influence or dominate others."

Shawn added, "Think about how much of ministry activity involves communication. It's part of nearly everything, but as we have seen this week, it is often siloed and disconnected. How is it, then, that most ministries' senior leadership teams do not have a seat for the Communications leader?"

## Championing a Mission-Driven Culture

As the conversation continued, the focus shifted naturally to the practicalities of embedding MHOS within each ministry's culture. The notion that Communications could play an equal, collaborative role with ministry and operational teams seemed to resonate, but with it came subtle fears rooted in culture change.

Greg shared a thought. "The mission itself demands unity and collaboration across every department, and messaging is crucial. It seems obvious when I hear you say it now, but I must admit I hadn't given this idea a thought before today."

"Every team has a unique role in helping fulfill that purpose," Shawn added, "and when any one team's insights are overlooked, the mission is affected. Communication is unique from a strategic perspective just because virtually nothing happens apart from it."

Matt added, "We're advocating for a model where your Communications leader's strategic insight connects the dots across all areas of ministry, ensuring every effort aligns with the mission. This doesn't mean that traditional ministry roles need to run everything by the Comms Director. As I hope you see now, true strategic collaboration in MissionHive is rooted in the Hive Effect where everyone is on the same page."

Emily, processing this, nodded thoughtfully. "So, by positioning Communications leaders at the strategic table, we're enabling those with the broadest view of our messaging to shape it from the beginning of our strategic planning, not just when they are fulfilling content requests?"

"Precisely," Shawn said. "It's about creating a culture where communication is integral—not as a secondary function but as a unifying voice that helps every department operate in harmony."

Greg looked around the mostly empty room, reflecting on the unity and hopefulness he had seen forming among his colleagues during the previous days. "I'm thinking about when our teams began learning the Hive Effect. It is clear how much stronger we are when we work together, and I see how this alignment could shape *everything* we do."

Each leader recognized that this cultural shift was both a challenge and an opportunity that would require trust and intentionality to bring to life.

## Clarifying Authority and Changing Culture

Greg broke the silence, voicing a question that had been on his mind. Where does authority lie within MHOS? Collaboration sounds great, but how do we ensure senior leadership can still make the final call in the moments that there isn't unity?"

Matt nodded, recognizing Greg's concern. "MissionHive doesn't diminish authority; it grounds it in mission alignment and shared accountability. Senior leadership still safeguards the mission's Identity and boundaries by leading from the front, but MHOS empowers teams to own their responsibilities without micromanagement. This is a culture shift that will take time."

Shawn added, "Accountability is central to MHOS. Trusting teams to execute their roles raises expectations for growth and support, not punishment. Feedback loops and assessments create a culture of learning and improvement, keeping everyone aligned and adapting."

Emily, listening intently, nodded in agreement. "That makes sense.

We're reframing authority as trust and accountability. That's a shift, but it feels essential for how we want FaithLink to grow."

"Exactly," Shawn affirmed. "And this kind of accountability, grounded in feedback and mission-focused improvement, builds confidence at all levels over time. By empowering people to do their best work, with leadership focused on the mission and its boundaries, the whole team operates with unity, trust, and a commitment to growth."

Greg looked at John and Maya, considering how this approach would enhance rather than compete with his leadership. "This feels different—like shared ownership with accountability as the anchor. I can see how this would prevent the missteps we've had with overlapping priorities."

Emily asked, "So practically, what other steps can we take to embed MHOS within our culture?" How do we make sure it's more than just another initiative?"

Matt responded, "MHOS should become the rhythm of daily operations, with each department supporting the mission uniquely. Communications staff will help explain and implement the Hive Effect, and ministry teams will continue to focus on what they do best. Both will benefit from greater operational collaboration."

Shawn continued, "Each team should see themselves as mission stewards within the MissionHive system. Every team aligns without overreaching, allowing every area to flourish collaboratively in their areas of expertise."

Emily nodded, "That feels empowering."

"Exactly! And when it all clicks," joked Matt, "you'll swear we planned it this way from the start."

## Final Reflections

As the first discussion of the day came to a close, Shawn and Matt invited the group to share their personal takeaways.

Greg spoke first, "What strikes me is how MHOS calls for unity at every level. Seeing each part of the ministry as essential to the mission makes it easier to prioritize. This clarity gives us confidence to say 'yes' to what aligns and 'no' to what doesn't reflect our missional Identity."

John added, "I see the power in this. MHOS isn't just a set of rules—it's a philosophy that influences every decision we make. For Communications, it's a reminder that our work shapes how the mission is perceived by everyone it touches—done well or poorly. We all want to do it well."

Emily smiled, "For me, mission-first thinking simplifies everything. At FaithLink, we've sometimes struggled to connect our fieldwork with our internal goals. MHOS makes it clear we're all working toward the same purpose. Structure doesn't ensure this works; good communication does."

Maya nodded in agreement, adding, "Recognizing Communications as strategic is refreshing. It's empowering to know my team's work can shape the mission's direction and help every team stay aligned. That's a level of purpose I've always hoped for in this role."

Shawn closed with a final thought,"What if every interaction in your organization reflected alignment with this mindset? MHOS is a commitment to staying grounded in your mission and values, in every decision. Each of you has the power to champion a culture that fulfills your calling with clarity and purpose."

The group had a clearer vision of how MissionHive OS would guide their next steps, each leader feeling prepared to champion this shift in their own unique roles.

### Aha Moment

By shifting from hierarchical control to mission-driven alignment, both HRCC and FaithLink discovered the joy of empowering every individual. MHOS elevates communication to a strategic role, fosters shared ownership, and balances accountability with collaboration. This alignment drives unity while preserving strong leadership, showcasing MissionHive's strength as a transformative system.

### Reflect & Apply

As you reflect on today's discussion, consider how your organization could benefit from mission-aligned empowerment. How can you ensure Communications plays a strategic role in fostering accountability, trust, and collaboration across teams?

## CHAPTER TWELVE
# Empowering Communications

*"The key for successful personal relationships and ministry is to understand and accept others as having a viewpoint as worthy of consideration as our own."*

**Duane Elmer**

The group of six reconvened, refreshed from a coffee break and ready to explore the unique role of the Communications team within the MHOS framework. Shawn started off by revisiting the staff Archetype in order to highlight its importance.

Shawn began, "Staff is one of the most critical Archetypes in any mission-driven organization, especially those where strategic alignment is vital. The reality is, without intentional focus, staff members can end up working toward different goals, sometimes even competing ones, due to siloed communication and isolated messaging. We have discussed this extensively this week."

Matt added, "In MHOS, alignment doesn't stop with senior leadership. It must move through every level to include each and every staff member. And that's where the Communications team plays a strategic role—not just in the messaging, but in the alignment itself. Communications ensures that every part of the staff team is aligned with the mission."

Greg was mostly tracking, but asked a clarifying question. "If I'm getting this right, you're saying that our Communications team essentially becomes the primary bridge between senior leadership's strategic direction and the day-to-day actions of our staff?"

"That is indeed what we are saying," Shawn replied. "Without Communications in a strategic role, even a well-aligned mission can get distorted as it moves through the organization. The Communications team helps clarify *'why'* and *'for whom'* each strategic goal is set. This isn't about telling pastors and ministry leaders how to speak, think, or act, but rather it's about ensuring that all actions and messages point back to the agreed-upon mission."

Emily jumped in. "If we're not all hearing the same strategic message as an organization, even unintentionally, we risk deviating from our core purpose."

Matt continued, "That's precisely it. In the MissionHive OS, communications isn't just about messaging—it's about *ensuring alignment*. Messaging is what people see on the surface—a website update, an email, a social media post—but alignment is what gives those messages depth and coherence. It's making sure every message reflects the mission, values, and goals of the organization. Without alignment, you end up with fragmented efforts—messages that might sound good in isolation but fail to connect with the bigger picture."

He paused to let the idea sink in before continuing, "Think of alignment as the thread that ties everything together. When communications are aligned, they don't just inform—they unify. They ensure that every ministry, every staff member, and every initiative is pulling in the same direction. It's not just about what we say, but why and how we say it, so that everyone, from the congregation to the staff, feels connected to the mission. That's the difference between a message and a movement."

Greg raised a concern. "But didn't you say this morning that Communications doesn't tell the ministry teams what to do or what to say? How is this idea compatible rather than conflicting?"

Shawn fielded the question, "We did say that, and it remains true. Because the Communications team takes an important role teaching and implementing the Hive Effect's elements on behalf of the senior leadership team, they are teaching each staff member, and even key volunteers, how to ensure that messages and activities are purposeful. At times, the Communications team should assist with messaging-especially in the early days of MHOS implementation-but over time these decisions will become more intuitive for everyone if true collaboration is happening. If ministry teams rush into tactical action without stopping to apply the Hive Effect's principles, you will still have breakdowns and silos. Whether at the beginning or years from now, you have to bring accountability and education to those situations to prevent misalignment or scope creep. This is the principle of constant organizational improvement. "

## The Role of Communications in Preventing Scope Creep

Maya shared a candid example from her experience. "In the past, we've pursued initiatives that seemed like great opportunities but were outside our core mission. At the time, they felt worthwhile, but we later realized they had pulled us away from our primary objectives." She paused, her tone turning reflective. "It's tough to admit, but we've lost valuable time, resources—and even donors—when we've strayed from our core mission."

Shawn responded, "This is a common issue, and honestly it's where Communications plays an essential role. MHOS, with the Hive Effect, is designed to prevent this kind of *scope creep*. When the organization operates strategically, it ensures that initiatives align with the mission. If an idea or project is outside that scope—even if it's noble—it's better for the organization to say, "Not yet," or to partner with other organizations whose mission is focused on that activity. This allows each team within your organization to stay laser-focused on your declared purpose."

Matt chimed in to reinforce the point. "Greg, in a church context, this often means taking a thoughtful look at peripheral ministries—those that are valuable but might not align fully with your core mission. For instance," Matt continued, "let's say a few students start hanging around after school because their parents work late, and someone in student ministry decides to launch an after-school program just for them. It's a noble idea, no doubt, but is it truly on mission? Is it the best use of your church's resources? If not, then it is important to ask if there is already an organization in town whose core mission is providing Christian after-school programs. They're purpose-built for that work. Partnering with them could make more sense than stretching your ministry to create something new for a smaller group, while still providing for the students and keeping your team freed up to pursue the church's mission activities."

"This is where the Hive Effect comes into play," Matt continued. "A Communications team often has a unique vantage point, with visibility across every ministry and initiative. When a request comes through their desk for a promotion or campaign, it's a signal to step back and ask the strategic questions: 'Does this fit within the mission senior leadership has set? Does it align with our mission Identity, or is it pulling us off course?' In this role, Communications isn't just a production shop—they're essential guardians of mission clarity."

Greg nodded in understanding but still had questions. "So, if a new opportunity comes up, it's not Communications' job to block it. But they are positioned to ask the initial strategic questions, then to ask the requesting team or senior leadership to determine if it aligns with our core mission. Is that right?"

"Exactly," Matt affirmed. "When Communications steps into this strategic role, they become an indispensable asset to senior leadership—not as gatekeepers shutting down ideas, but as guardians of the mission. By putting the mission first, they transform from a production shop into a frontline filter, ensuring activities, messaging, and relationships align with the core mission."

Matt continued, "Even well-intentioned ideas can sometimes stray off-mission. Over time, though, every team, office, region, or campus will develop the same commitment to protecting and fulfilling the mission. For this reason, the permission to say "No" is vital."

## Avoiding Silos Through Unified Messaging Channels

As the heads were nodding in understanding, Shawn kept the conversation moving, adding the next layer to the discussion. "One of the most common forms of silo-building in larger ministries is through decentralized messaging. Each area of ministry—whether it's a major team like campuses at Harvest Ridge, regional teams at FaithLink, or even smaller segments like student ministries—often creates its own messaging channels. They develop separate social media accounts, newsletters, and sometimes even independent websites or apps. And while well-intentioned, this can create massive, unwanted complexity."

Matt glanced at Shawn, who gave a knowing smile, anticipating what was coming next. "Shawn and I worked with a large multi-site church that had—wait for it—56 social media accounts," Matt said, pausing to let the weight of that number settle in. He leaned back with a grin and added, "And those were just the ones we knew about."

Shawn chimed in, "I worked with an international ministry that went through several cycles of centralizing and decentralizing. Over time they ended up with different logos for each global region, disconnected regional channels and audience segments, and very siloed communications. This was hurting the entire Identity of the ministry because people, especially donors, no longer knew if they were one organization or multiple."

Emily nodded, realizing how true this was. "I can see how that splinters communication for our audiences. People start having to chase down information, piecing it together across channels, or worse get the same messaging a bunch of times, just from different departments"

"Exactly," Shawn agreed. "For the Archetypes we serve, fractured communication quickly becomes frustrating. Instead of clear, consistent messaging delivered through relationally managed channels, they're hit with a chaotic churn of disconnected updates from various teams or segments. "Even worse," Shawn continued, "your organization is just one of many competing for space in their phones and inboxes. When communication is disjointed, you're not cutting through the noise—you're adding to it. We call this the *Swarm Effect*."

He paused, letting the phrase settle in before elaborating. "In nature, a swarm of bees is actually purposeful. It may appear chaotic and disorienting, but every bee is operating in alignment with the colony's needs—relocating to a new hive or responding to a specific situation. The swarm, while overwhelming to the outsider, is organized and directed. But when it comes to ministry communication, a swarm created by silos loses this alignment. Instead of appearing organized, it feels chaotic to those we are messaging. Archetypes like Parents, Field Volunteers, and Seekers no longer see the organization as a unified body working toward a shared mission. They see and feel chaos, and worse, they feel like we don't see or know them."

Shawn continued, "Let's take the Parent Archetype as an example. A parent at Harvest Ridge might receive separate communications about children's ministry events, volunteer opportunities, and upcoming small groups. If they are deeply involved, they are also getting messages on giving. Each message is created with good intentions, but the cumulative effect overwhelms them. They feel swarmed. Instead of helping them stay connected, it adds stress to their already busy lives, making it harder for them to engage."

Matt jumped in, "Now imagine a Field Volunteer at FaithLink. They're on the ground, deeply connected to your mission, but they're inundated with communication that doesn't always speak to their context. Updates from headquarters, regional partnership news, general donor-focused newsletters—portions of it feels irrelevant to their specific involvement. How often are they learning information indirectly rather than through meaningful conversations with staff leaders? Over time, they will tune out or disengage because they don't feel seen or understood."

Shawn added, "And that's the problem. When siloed teams send messages independently and without coordination, there's no alignment. The messaging might seem organized in your silo, but to the Archetypes, it's a chaotic flood. They don't see the organization's purpose or mission in these communications—they only see disconnection. I say all the time that while people onboard, they rarely offboard. They just disappear."

John sat forward with interest. "So, the Swarm Effect isn't just about the amount of communication—it's about how fragmented it feels when it comes from different directions."

"Exactly," Shawn affirmed. "The Swarm Effect happens when we prioritize the quantity of communication over the alignment and quality of the message. If we find our teams add channels because it feels easy for us to control what we want to say, it is a warning sign that someone is going rogue in their own tactical silo. Too many channels, reactive habits, and a lack of strategic collaboration create noise instead of clarity. And this affects every Archetype-even Staff. Communications staff understand this issue and can help protect against it by providing other solutions through strategic dialogue."

Matt added, "The key is to streamline communication through the Hive Effect. When all messaging flows from a unified mission and respects the unique journeys of your Archetypes, communication transforms. Instead of chaos, you get clarity. Instead of disengagement, you get connection. The touchpoints in the Archetype journeys inform us where to meet people effectively."

Shawn nodded. "With the Hive Effect, Archetypes like a Disciple or a Partner Organization can see clear pathways to engage and belong, rather than competing messages pulling them in different directions. When you embrace this framework, your communication becomes a signal—a clear, unified call to participate in the beecosystem—not a swarm that overwhelms."

John, his enthusiasm growing, offered, "I can see how this convergence doesn't mean we lose the distinct voice of each ministry team. But it does ensure that the messaging across the board remains aligned with the mission and that our audiences aren't forced to track multiple sources to stay connected."

"Exactly," Shawn agreed. "The result? Your Archetypes feel seen and valued as participants in the mission, rather than feeling overwhelmed. We want to hear people say, 'It's like you knew what I needed before I did!'"

## Elevating the Communications Team Without Undermining Others

"Another important factor here is balance," Shawn said. "Empowering Communications doesn't mean we're diminishing anyone else's role. Every team has a mission-critical part to play in MHOS. Pastors, ministry leaders, and operational staff each bring unique expertise to serving the people entrusted to their care. Communications staff simply helps senior leadership ensure alignment across these functions."

Emily looked relieved. "That's a concern I had—Communications stepping in as a central authority might lead some staff to feel their contributions are being undermined."

"It's a valid concern," Matt agreed, "but MHOS is designed to prevent that by fostering collaboration and alignment. It's not Communications versus everyone else—it's everyone working together. Think of the hive again: different types of bees, each with a specific function, all working in harmony to produce the best honey with remarkable efficiency. Communications doesn't overshadow other roles; it amplifies and aligns the messaging so that everyone stays on the same page, working toward a shared purpose, with every Archetype in every Environment."

John voiced a concern. "So what happens when the messaging styles and goals just don't align? That still happens, right?"

Shawn confirmed, "Yes, it still happens. But MissionHive provides the framework to overcome those disconnects. Collaboration is not the absence of conflict. In fact, I believe many forms of conflict and disagreement are helpful. They cause us to talk about things rather than work around them. Remember, this isn't about Communications having control; it's about keeping focused. Communications helps each part of the ministry understand and communicate the mission without straying into territory outside that scope. In those moments where we can't agree, as long as ownership is defined, a final decision must be made and the owner is accountable for their decision. When Communications staff defer, they can't come running back with "I told you that wouldn't work" if something fails. The reverse is also true. We have to learn to work through conflict and find joy in experimentation."

## Empowering Communications

Maya voiced a final concern. "How do we all embrace this type of strategic cooperation without getting overwhelmed by the daily pulse of ministry?"

Matt addressed this directly. "Communications, especially in MHOS, doesn't sit on the sidelines just offering advice. They don't become mystic oracles in a back room!" he said, laughing. "They are integral partners, directly engaged in every step of mission alignment. Their focus on the Hive Effect means they're not just transmitting information but actively involved in understanding each ministry's needs, addressing concerns, and refining messaging in real time. *But this has to work both ways.* Just as Communications respects the expertise and decisions of ministry teams, it's crucial for ministry teams to recognize and value the strategic expertise that Communications brings to the table."

John chimed in. "That's the challenge, isn't it? We can only accomplish this if Communications is respected as a key partner. We're not here to impose ideas or override ministry decisions, but to ensure the mission is clear and actionable for everyone. At the same time, there's a history of Communications being treated as a service desk—our strategic input often gets sidelined, and that marginalization creates a disconnect."

"Unfortunately, that happens a lot," Shawn said. "This is where we tackle one of the unspoken tensions in many organizations. Communications roles aren't about telling people how to minister, just like ministry leaders aren't telling Communications how to craft campaign strategy or align messaging across channels. The expertise of each team must be acknowledged and leveraged. When that mutual respect is present, it fosters collaboration rather than competition. The Hive Effect is designed to create that alignment—not just in messaging but in trust and shared purpose."

Matt added, "Think of it this way: the insights from ministry teams inform that alignment just as much as Communications helps amplify it. When both sides see themselves as contributors to the same mission, you move from operating in silos, from holding on to petty territorialism, to working in sync."

With everyone happy but hungry after a long morning, Shawn brought the session to a close with one last thought before lunch, "the Hive Effect ensures that everyone—not just senior leadership—understands the mission and how to act on it. It prevents silos, builds trust and respect, and keeps everyone accountable to the same purpose. That's how you move from functioning as separate teams to operating as one unified body, all working together to fulfill your mission."

### Aha Moment

Communications staff are essential, mission-minded staff wholly engaged in ministry, not merely serving as support teams. They play a vital role in keeping activity and messaging aligned with the mission, preventing silos and scope creep. They work with senior leadership as enablers of the Hive Effect for the entire ministry.

### Reflect & Apply

Identify ways to empower your own Communications team within your organization's mission-driven framework. How can they be strategic partners in amplifying your vision?

### Important Note

While not every organization has a dedicated Communications Director, the role of communication remains essential. In smaller churches or ministries, this responsibility may fall to a pastor, executive leader, or even a gifted volunteer. What matters is that someone with influence understands how communication shapes culture, alignment, and mission clarity. The principles in this book apply regardless of team size—what's needed is intentionality. Organizational communications is more than a department; it's a discipline that deserves leadership-level attention.

# CHAPTER THIRTEEN

# Breaking Down Silos through Collaboration

*"In most situations, silos rise up not because of what executives are doing purposefully but rather because of what they are failing to do: provide themselves and their employees with a compelling context for working together."*

**Patrick Lencioni**

After the lunch break, the group returned to the room, energized and ready to tackle one of the most critical aspects of MHOS: fostering a collaborative, unified culture that dismantles silos. Shawn set the tone for the session.

"Earlier, we touched on how silos can form when organizations lack strategic alignment," Shawn began, sitting back in his chair. "Now, let's take that conversation further. Silos are something that happen in every organization as it grows. At their best, silos serve a practical purpose—they allow teams to specialize and focus on specific areas. But when those silos harden, they stop being helpful and start creating barriers. Departments protect their territories rather than working toward a unified mission, and that's when *high-functioning dysfunction* sets in."

Shawn's words sank in quickly as each of the leaders reflected on how silos had affected their own organizations.

Emily nodded. "I've seen this at FaithLink. We each have our areas, and while we're all on the same mission, sometimes it feels like we're each speaking different languages. I've been here since college. I've seen staff come and go, but for the most part, silos seem to always be a challenge we wrestle with."

"Wow," Matt said, recognizing that Emily had just uncovered one of the most perilous expressions of siloed organizations. "That's where silos can become *sacred cows*—assumptions or practices people feel they can't challenge because the practices themselves have been around so long or because they provide a sense of stability. But these sacred cows are likely blocking your organization from achieving its potential."

Shawn seized the moment to unpack the concept of sacred cows within the context of MissionHive, grounding it in biblical history. "The term *sacred cow* actually has its roots in the Bible, specifically in the book of Exodus," he began. "While Moses was on Mount Sinai receiving the Ten Commandments from God, the Israelites grew impatient. They couldn't handle the waiting, so they decided to take matters into their own hands." Shawn paused, letting the weight of the story settle. "They melted down their gold and fashioned a golden calf to worship. That's where the idea of a sacred cow originates— something man made, given undue reverence, that pulls us away from the true mission."

Matt stepped in, building on the point. "The sacred cow term is not meant as a critique of ministry leaders or teams. The truth is, as humans, we're all wired to crave purpose, value, and action. Sometimes, though," he said, pausing for effect, "in our impatience or busyness, we end up elevating practices or traditions that no longer serve the mission. The key is recognizing when it's time to recalibrate and get back on track."

Greg was intrigued. "How do we identify these sacred cows?"

Shawn smiled, ready for the question. "That's a great question," he said. "It starts with analyzing our assumptions—challenging the practices and traditions we hold onto without asking why. It's about having the courage to ask difficult questions, like 'Does this still serve our mission, or is it just familiar?' Matt and I call this *sacred cow tipping*."

The room broke into laughter at the phrase, and Shawn shared a lighthearted anecdote. "Okay, let me explain. Both Matt and I grew up in the Midwest, surrounded by small farm towns with not much to do. Now, rumor has it that cows sleep standing up, so the legend goes that kids would tip them over at night and run away—although, for the record, neither of us ever tried it."

The group burst into laughter again, the humor helping everyone relate to the idea. "But here's the thing," he continued, his tone turning reflective. "Sacred-cow tipping in ministry context is different—it's about intentionally challenging what's become untouchable and asking whether it's still mission-aligned. Sometimes, what feels stable is actually holding us back. And in times of change, people may seize onto sacred cows without realizing they are doing it. This is the pinnacle of silos and misalignment. They provide a false sense of security and safety that may be detrimental to the mission."

Matt continued, "This goes hand-in-hand with the culture of *collaboration*. In MHOS, collaboration is about more than just working together—it's about cultivating a shared culture of learning and cooperation. Everyone is a messenger, not just the Communications team. We must create shared language and unity of purpose, regardless of our departments."

He continued, "Part of this shared culture means embracing feedback and engaging in what we call *positively-charged diagnostics*. We need to create an atmosphere where healthy criticism isn't only accepted but encouraged. It's like a battery: without polarity—positive and negative—you don't get any power."

Greg, processing the idea, asked, "So how do we give this kind of feedback without causing friction?"

"This is where constructive dialogue and diagnostics come in," Shawn shared. "We've developed a formula that helps identify areas where dysfunction might be high-functioning in disguise. We'll unpack it together, but remember: this isn't about pointing fingers. It's about recognizing patterns and finding solutions."

Shawn walked to the whiteboard at the front of the room, writing three phrases in bold letters: "Tactics Before Strategy," "False Consensus Effect," and "Cycles of Responsiveness." Turning to the group, he said, "One of the reasons silos persist—even in organizations with clear missions—is what we call High-Functioning Dysfunction."

He paused, allowing the phrase to sink in before continuing. "High-Functioning Dysfunction isn't chaos. It's the kind of 'busy productivity' that looks effective on the surface but drains resources, misaligns teams, and ultimately misses the mission. Let me briefly outline three contributing dynamics that often drive it."

Shawn pointed to the first element. "First, Tactics Before Strategy (TbS). This happens when we prioritize action before the intentionality of asking 'Why are we doing this?' or 'Who are we doing it for?' It creates a cycle of constant busyness without meaningful progress."

Next, he tapped the second phrase. "False Consensus Effect (FCE) is the assumption that everyone else sees things the way we do, leading to communication gaps and misaligned expectations. We touched on this earlier this week in the context of Archetypes. This one is sneaky because it can even make us over-communicate, drowning our audiences in irrelevant messaging."

Finally, Shawn underlined the last phrase. "And then there's Cycles of Responsiveness (CoR). This happens when teams become so reactive to problems or urgent needs that they lose sight of proactive planning. It's like spinning plates—eventually, something crashes."

Shawn stepped back quietly, giving the leaders a moment to absorb the concepts. "We'll unpack these shortly as we explore how diagnostics can help your teams collaborate more effectively. But for now, I want you to start recognizing where these dynamics might already exist in your organization. When we "add" them together," he said, stepping back to the white board and writing under the line he drew a moment ago, "the result is a culture of High-Functioning Dysfunction (HfD)."

"These dynamics don't exist in isolation," Matt added. "When they converge, they create a culture that looks busy but lacks alignment. Like Shawn said, we will return to this formula shortly in more detail. For now, just keep it in mind as we discuss how to foster collaboration and break down silos."

## Building a New Culture

Shawn continued by emphasizing that a truly collaborative culture requires more than surface-level alignment. "What we're after isn't just logistical cooperation; it's a culture where every team genuinely understands the mission and feels empowered to pursue it creatively within shared guidelines. This isn't something that can be achieved by adding more meetings or 'top-down' directives."

Greg nodded. "It sounds like you're talking about creating a space where meetings involve people who are mission-driven and strategically aligned, not just following a checklist."

"100% correct, Greg," Shawn replied. "When alignment becomes embedded in the culture, it no longer feels like compliance. It feels like ownership. We need to shift from thinking of alignment as a task to thinking of alignment as part of our DNA. That way, collaboration becomes natural and intuitive, not an afterthought or post-mortem following a failed initiative."

Emily felt cautious. "Shifting culture is always ambitious and daunting-especially with ingrained practices and sacred cows as you mentioned before. But I think as you have outlined it, FaithLink staff will find it healing."

Shawn smiled. "When we begin to challenge these sacred cows, people often feel threatened—not because they're resistant to improvement, but because these things provide a sense of stability in times of change. You're right about the healing. In fact, even in corporate America, people will gladly take less money to work in a healthy organization that is making a difference in the world. I believe ministries should be setting the standard in this area. That's a topic for another day," he said, stepping off his imaginary soapbox.

Matt stepped in, "This process isn't about dismissing our feelings to build a new reality either. It's about acknowledging them and guiding people toward finding security in a shared mission rather than clinging to outdated practices. In MHOS, the goal is to foster adaptability—empowering people to feel safe, even as old methods are re-evaluated, and let go."

He added with a grin, "Think of it like Indiana Jones swapping out the treasure for a bag of sand before the pressure plate reacts. We're not destroying anyone's ambition or purpose; we're simply guiding it to align more closely with the mission. When approached thoughtfully, sacred cow tipping can be a much smoother process than you'd expect."

John nodded. "So, it's about providing people with a purpose-focused framework they can depend on, rather than simply saying, 'Here's a new way. Follow it.'"

"Yes," Matt agreed, "and this brings us back to the idea that communications isn't just a department, it's part of the organization's shared culture. In MissionHive, everyone is a flag bearer. Every team, from ministry to operations, plays a role in how the mission is conveyed. Collaboration becomes the standard, not the exception."

## Empowerment and Innovation: Foundations for Collaboration

Shawn continued, "To break down silos, we need more than a cooperative attitude. Collaboration thrives in an atmosphere of empowerment and innovation. When staff feel they're trusted and their contributions are valued, they're more likely to bring forward creative, mission-aligned ideas."

Maya glanced thoughtfully at Emily. "So, it's not just about doing things together. It's about allowing each person to bring their best ideas forward without feeling they have to get 'permission' at every step."

Shawn nodded. "Exactly, Maya. Empowerment means giving people the space to experiment within the boundaries of the mission. When each person feels empowered to act in alignment with the organization's core purpose, collaboration becomes natural. And innovation becomes an organic part of how you approach challenges."

John asked, "In practice, though, how does that work? Especially with so many teams—some working on day-to-day tasks and others, like Communications, guiding larger, organization-wide initiatives but also day-to-day activities."

Matt took this one. "Empowerment doesn't mean freedom from accountability. It means every team is equipped to make mission-aligned decisions within its expertise. For example, if Communications is developing a strategy that impacts ministry outreach, then ministry teams can trust that Communications has considered how it fits into the wider mission, and vice versa. We foster innovation by building trust that each team's actions support a unified strategy, rather than competing agendas. And hopefully, we're not making strategies in isolation, but through dialogue and shared investment in the planning."

Emily added, "So, we're fostering both independence and trust—that any team will deliver strategically and not just tactically?"

"Yes," Matt said. "It's a collaborative autonomy, in many respects. When each team feels empowered, silos start to dissolve because people are encouraged to think beyond their own tasks and see how their work impacts the whole organization. It's a shift to proactive communication and mutual ownership."

Greg nodded and confirmed out loud. "We're working toward a mindset where every team trusts that other teams are working within the mission scope—and that each team is equally committed to supporting the entire ministry's goals. And if they are not, we have accountability discussions and get back on track."

Shawn and Matt nodded in agreement.

## Positively Charged Diagnostics: Cultivating a Healthy, Collaborative Culture

Shawn transitioned, building on the earlier introduction of the formula for High-Functioning Dysfunction: Tactics Before Strategy (TbS) + False Consensus Effect (FCE) + Cycles of Responsiveness (CoR) = High-Functioning Dysfunction (HfD).

"You are seeing now that these diagnostics," he explained while pointing again to the white board, "are practical tools to help us assess whether we're fostering a collaborative culture or unintentionally reinforcing silos. Let's dig deeper into each element, understanding how they affect alignment."

## Tactics Before Strategy (TbS)

"When our actions focus on tactics instead of strategy," Shawn said, "we end up checking boxes rather than achieving meaningful outcomes. In our meetings and planning sessions, we need to ask, 'Why are we doing this, and for whom?'—questions rooted in the Hive Effect."

Greg nodded. "It's about ensuring that strategy—not just actionable tasks—drives our activity."

"Exactly," Shawn replied. "When we prioritize strategy, our conversations focus on the core mission. It aligns us with the bigger picture and keeps us from falling into endless tactical busywork. The goal isn't just productivity; it's productivity with purpose. For some reason, staff are often eager to jump straight into action—to the tasks—which can create friction and problems down the road. Without a strategic plan to guide those efforts, tasks carried out in silos can lead to misalignment and inefficiencies. True collaboration begins when strategy sets the foundation, ensuring that every action serves a unified mission rather than isolated priorities."

Matt added, "And don't overthink strategy like it is a grandiose plan that takes weeks to develop. An effective strategy simply needs to address the three elements of the Hive Effect, and then tasks can be designed that are effective."

## False Consensus Effect (FCE)

"The second diagnostic tool, the False Consensus Effect, is one of the most subtle yet damaging barriers to collaboration," Shawn explained. "It's the assumption that others share our perspectives or understandings when they don't. This disconnect leads to miscommunication, ineffective messaging, and missed opportunities."

He continued, "FCE isn't just about assuming our audience understands us—it's also about assuming we fully understand them. When organizations think they know their community without engaging deeply, they risk missing what truly matters to the people they're serving. For example, if FaithLink assumes that all General Donors are primarily motivated by field reports and data, they may overlook the emotional connection many donors seek through stories of impact. It's easy to misstep when assumptions replace relational understanding."

Matt emphasized, "FCE is a two-way disconnect. On one hand, we assume Archetypes understand our mission and values as deeply as we do. On the other hand, we assume we know their needs, motivations, and pain points without truly listening or asking. Both lead to breakdowns in communication and engagement."

Maya chimed in, reflecting on FaithLink's challenges. "That sounds like what happens when we use insider language. We assume donors and volunteers know the acronyms we throw around, but they don't—and that creates a barrier instead of building connection."

"Great example," Shawn affirmed. "And the other side of that coin is thinking we've nailed our messaging without ever asking the Archetypes if it resonates. FCE doesn't just affect external communication—it can divide internal teams, too. When leaders assume alignment without checking for it, silos form. Departments start working at cross-purposes because they interpret things differently or their definitions of success differ."

He concluded, "Breaking FCE requires humility. Whether it's understanding your Archetypes better or clarifying internal alignment, the key is asking questions, seeking feedback, and engaging in dialogue. Archetypes aren't static—they grow, change, and respond differently depending on where they are in their journey. If we're not intentional about seeing through their lens, we'll always miss opportunities to connect."

## Cycles of Responsiveness (CoR)

"Cycles of Responsiveness may sound positive," Shawn said, "but unhealthy cycles of responsiveness are what this term refers to. Ad hoc meetings, endless 'urgent' adjustments, and constant corrective reaction can easily overtake the strategic work we need to focus on. It creates a reactive culture that spins in circles, exhausting everyone involved."

Matt interjected with a smile, "And let's be honest—have you ever experienced a team working hard on their event, only to realize 40% of what should have been in place wasn't ready because they didn't reach out to other teams in the organization?"

Greg chuckled, exchanging a glance with Emily. "Are you kidding? That's a weekly occurrence!" The room laughed, recognizing the all-too-familiar pattern.

"Exactly," Matt replied. "True collaboration means not only anticipating our audience's needs but also working cohesively within our own teams to prevent last-minute scrambles. When we connect proactive strategy with our shared expertise within the Hive Effect, we don't just get things done—we do things well."

| MISSION HIVE OS | HFD FORMULA: DIAGNOSTICS |
| --- | --- |
|  | Tactics Before Strategy (TbS) |
| + | False Consensus Effect (FcE) |
| + | Cycles of Responsiveness (CoR) |
| = |  |
|  | High-Functioning Dysfunction (HfD) |

## High-Functioning Dysfunction (HfD)

"Now, let's connect the dots," Shawn said, bringing the focus back to the formula. "When these dynamics—TbS, FCE, and CoR—are unchecked, they combine to create High-Functioning Dysfunction. It's 'high-functioning' because, on the surface, everything looks productive. But beneath that productivity is a fragile ecosystem, stretched thin and misaligned. Fragile ecosystems are bad. Healthy beecosystems are good."

He paused, letting the room reflect. "Here's the good news: HfD isn't permanent. It can be undone by working backwards to address the root causes. If you replace tactics-first thinking with strategy, bridge gaps caused by FCE, and break unhealthy CoR cycles, you can dismantle HfD. The goal is to create a healthy beecosystem where productivity and alignment reinforce one another instead of pulling in opposite directions."

Matt wrapped up with a practical takeaway: "These diagnostics aren't about blame—they're about insight. They help us see where we're stuck so we can move forward with clarity and alignment. When every team member commits to fostering a mission-first culture, alignment isn't just a goal—it becomes your way of operating."

Shawn and Matt gave a few minutes for each leader to reflect on their own experiences with TbS, FCE, and CoR. They could see where High-Functioning Dysfunction had subtly crept into their work, often disguised as productivity. But now, they were equipped with a framework to turn those challenges into pathways for unity and shared purpose.

## Sacred-Cow Tipping: Overcoming Entrenched Practices for Mission Alignment

Matt broke the silence for the next part of the discussion with a smile. "Now, let's circle back to sacred cows."

The team shared a few chuckles, loving the concept and each imagining ways to casually drop it into conversations back at the office.

Matt continued, "Sacred cows are often the practices or systems we feel attached to because they've 'always been done this way.' They seem harmless but can easily create resistance when you're trying to realign toward a mission-first strategy."

"Here's the challenge," Matt continued. "To break down silos and foster collaboration, we have to identify these sacred cows and ask ourselves: 'Do they genuinely serve the mission, or are they simply comfortable habits?'"

Greg was intrigued. "How do we begin that process without stepping on a lot of toes, or hooves, in ways that cause friction?"

"It requires sensitivity," Shawn replied. "But it also requires courage. When we're engaging with something that's sensitive or even cherished, it's essential to lead with the mission. And this is where MissionHive becomes our guide. When everyone understands that the 'why' of MHOS is rooted in the mission, we can all begin to question what's sacred and what's strategic with a shared perspective."

Maya spoke up, reflecting on FaithLink's experience. "In our organization, I think we've developed sacred cows around certain messaging channels. We're so accustomed to relying on specific methods that it's difficult to imagine changing them. But looking at it through the lens of MissionHive, I realize that if those channels don't serve the Archetypes effectively, they're actually barriers."

"That's a great insight," Shawn said. "Every communication channel, event, and method of outreach should align with your mission. Sacred cows are often misaligned with that, precisely because they aren't questioned regularly. A practice becomes a sacred cow when it's maintained out of habit rather than mission alignment."

Matt turned back to the group, ready to provide a concrete exercise. "Here's what I want each of you to do: think of a practice in your organization that feels untouchable. It might be something no one questions because it's familiar. Then, ask yourself, 'How does this serve our mission, our Archetypes, and our strategic Environments? Would eliminating or adjusting it better align with the mission?'"

John raised his hand. "For us, I think a sacred cow is our approach to volunteer recruitment. We always rely on the same events, announcements and programs to engage potential volunteers, but it's not as effective as it could be. Changing it feels risky, but maybe that's the point."

"Precisely," Shawn replied. "If a method no longer supports the mission or serves the Archetypes effectively, it might be time to 'tip' it. Letting go of a practice isn't about rejecting its past value; it's about freeing your team to pursue methods that will best serve your mission in the future."

Emily shifted back, "This is intimidating to me because some of these practices feel like they define us now. When I took over the Executive Director role, I inherited so many sacred cows that I've wanted to change. But we can't go herd-tipping."

"That's a natural feeling," Matt assured her, "and I am stealing herd-tipping! Remember, this practice isn't about losing Identity. It's about finding ways to ensure that the practices and beliefs that define you truly support your core mission. We're not just questioning for the sake of change; we're assessing to make sure every choice aligns with the purpose you're here to fulfill. It is different when you inherit an organization, because there will be a tendency to want to "blow things up" and start over. That's poor change management, right? Make a plan, and if needed a timeline, to tip-over sacred cows at a pace your team can handle."

Greg seemed to be reflecting deeply, then said, "What if some of the things we need to 'tip' are the very practices that got us here in the first place? I planted Harvest Ridge-so I didn't inherit sacred cows in the way Emily did-but after 20 years we certainly have them."

Shawn responded gently, "Greg, that's often the case. The practices that served you well for a season might not be what you need for the future. Like everything else in life, your organization is continually evolving and adapting. It's about acknowledging that those practices were valuable but also recognizing when it's time to adapt. The mission remains constant. We should celebrate the end of something like we do the start of something new."

Matt nodded, smiling at the group. "And that, right there, is what a mission-first approach looks like. When you're willing to question everything—every practice, every event, every tradition—with an eye on the mission, you create a culture where collaboration thrives. Silos break down, and teams work together because they're all focused on the same ultimate purpose."

As the conversation settled, the team sensed a new energy in the room. It was clear that this would require courage, but they were ready to evaluate every "untouchable" part of their organization with fresh eyes, in service to a mission that was bigger than tradition or habit.

## Integrating Positively Charged Diagnostics for Collaborative Growth

With the group having introduced and explored the concept of diagnostics, Shawn encouraged the leaders. "There's something incredibly valuable," he began, "about applying these positively charged diagnostics to keep us consistently mission-aligned. These aren't just one-off feedback moments; they're ways to embed learning and alignment across every area."

John asked, "How do we ensure diagnostics stay empowering and don't become unhealthy criticism?"

"Good question," Shawn said with a smile. " Think back to our illustration of a battery that needs both positive and negative contact points to create power. A team needs honest assessments focused on growth rather than blame. The 'positive charge' comes from the way we frame these assessments—as a shared effort to keep moving forward together."

Matt added, "In that sense, we're talking about more than one approach. Diagnostics can happen through structured debriefs or ongoing feedback loops. When everyone understands that the purpose is alignment and innovation, the focus shifts from critique to shared mission. And innovation—well, that's one of the hardest things to keep alive in established organizations. There are risks, and innovation attempts might fail, but those attempts are essential. As long as you build in time to debrief, even challenges and setbacks can yield growth."

Greg nodded slowly, considering. "So we're looking at diagnostics as ongoing tools to check in with the mission. But what about when someone, or a team, feels targeted by this kind of feedback?"

"Important point," Shawn agreed. "That's why it's crucial to position diagnostics as a collective endeavor. When everyone knows we're working for mission success, diagnostics are seen as opportunities for growth, not baseless criticism. The longer an organization has existed, the more we find some teams have a higher number of sacred cows than others. There can be many reasons for this, but some teams will feel more in the crosshairs of diagnostic change. It's up to you as senior leaders to ensure the "why" is always clear, and walk alongside those teams with genuine care."

John added, "So, is this something we do in every meeting or just after major initiatives?"

"Both can work," Matt replied. "Regular check-ins are essential, but deeper evaluations happen at key points, like after a campaign or event. You might ask, 'What brought us closer to mission alignment?' or 'What can we adjust for even greater impact next time?' Over time, each organization will find the rhythm and style of diagnostics that work best."

## Reflecting on Silos, Sacred Cows, and Collaboration

As Matt and Shawn's week with the HRCC and FaithLink teams wound to an end, they encouraged the group to reflect on what they'd unpacked so far. Greg, Emily, John, and Maya exchanged glances and exhaled in unison, each sensing the potential of what they were learning, but tired from the deep thinking."

Shawn started, "We've covered a lot of ground. I know it might feel overwhelming, but real alignment requires everyone pulling together with a shared sense of purpose, not just following a system or checklist."

Matt added, "To reinforce that, I want to remind you all that MissionHive itself is a journey. Breaking down silos, identifying sacred cows, and creating a culture of collaboration doesn't happen overnight. But every small step you take brings you closer to a ministry that's truly mission-first."

Emily reflected, "I think what stands out most to me is the need to stay vigilant—constantly asking why we do things, being honest about where we might be clinging to outdated methods. It's a little uncomfortable, but it feels essential."

Matt jumped in, adding more perspective. "I'm not sure if any of you are familiar with a 12-step recovery process, but one of those steps involves taking a daily personal inventory—reflecting on your choices, any mistakes made, and the people affected along the way. While I'm not directly comparing that process to what we're doing here, there's a reason this kind of uncomfortable reflection is transformative. In a ministry context, that same principle of honest, ongoing evaluation can bring about healing and strengthen the health of the entire organization.

Shawn added, "MissionHive provides a framework that not only aids evaluation but also creates space for healing and growth within the organization. Alignment is an active, ongoing process—not a heavy burden on a few but a pathway to wholeness for all. When everyone understands their role within the mission, collaboration becomes natural, like different parts of the hive working in harmony. By addressing issues in real time, you don't just minimize dysfunction— you create opportunities for restoration and a renewed sense of purpose that can prevent problems from taking root."

Greg, visibly energized, nodded. "This is a full-culture shift. We're talking about changing the way we interact, how we plan, and even how we measure success."

Matt agreed. "That's right. Culture can be a buzzword, but when it's mission-driven and embedded at every level, it becomes the heart of an organization."

Shawn looked around the room, his tone steady. "Let's not forget the importance of learning to say 'no.' We have to protect the Identity and mission of the ministry. Not every good opportunity aligns with your core purpose, and as leaders, you have to have the clarity and courage to redirect efforts that could cause scope creep."

As the session wound down, Shawn and Matt looked at each leader, sensing both the inspiration and the challenges ahead. Greg and Emily, especially, wore expressions that mixed eagerness with the sober realization of the work required to create lasting change.

Shawn closed with a final thought. "As you step back into your ministries, remember that MissionHive values unity. Authority remains with you as leaders, but the input and expertise of every team member—including John and Maya—adds depth and direction to your decisions. This collaboration allows you to protect the mission without being the sole gatekeepers, empowering everyone to play a strategic role."

Matt added, "And keep this in mind: a collaborative culture is a resilient one. When everyone understands the mission and their unique contribution to it, you're building a ministry that isn't just effective—it's adaptable, sustainable, and ready for growth."

### Aha Moment

Each leader felt the transformative power of a collaborative, mission-driven culture. They saw how alignment, sacred-cow tipping, and empowering staff could move their ministries beyond high-functioning dysfunction to sustainable, unified impact.

### Reflect & Apply

Identify one "sacred cow" in your organization that may be hindering mission alignment. Discuss how letting it go could enhance collaboration and focus resources on what matters most.

# Part 6: Implementing MissionHive OS

## Hive Insight

Part 6 guides leaders in embedding MHOS principles into their organizational culture and daily operations, focusing on creating a unified, mission-driven community that aligns leadership, communications, and ministry teams. This part emphasizes practical application, empowering leaders to position the Hive Effect while fostering collaboration, accountability, and intentionality across all levels.

CHAPTER FOURTEEN

# Homework

*"If you want to go fast, go alone.*
*If you want to go far, go together."*

**African Proverb**

*"Coming together is a beginning,*
*staying together is progress,*
*and working together is success."*

**Henry Ford**


**W**ith a renewed sense of direction from the week-long MissionHive workshops, the HRCC and FaithLink teams returned to their respective organizations, fully aware of the significant task ahead. While Matt and Shawn had guided them through core MHOS principles, the responsibility to prepare their ministries for the cultural shift now rested on Greg, Emily, and their senior leadership teams.

## Presenting to the Boards

In both ministries, the initial steps centered around board approval. Greg at HRCC and Emily at FaithLink crafted executive reports that summarized the vision for adopting MHOS, with a focus on its core essentials: the *Hive Effect, the culture of collaboration,* and *positively charged diagnostics.*

At *HRCC*, Greg's report emphasized that MHOS would completely replace EOS as a more fitting, mission-centered operating system for ministry. He explained how the Hive Effect would create a cohesive framework, ensuring both top-down and bottom-up alignment that would reinforce the church's mission. The Hive Effect would also provide a strategic flow for communication that could reduce silos and enhance collaboration. He noted that while diagnostics were central to MHOS, he was still wrapping his mind around how to implement them in the day-to-day.

*Meanwhile, at FaithLink,* Emily tailored her executive summary to address her board's misunderstandings about MissionHive requiring a full restructuring. She explained that MHOS does not require altering the existing organizational structure; rather, it operates effectively within any structure, including FaithLink's globally dispersed model. Emily emphasized that MHOS would bring consistency and cohesion to communications and ministry efforts across regional teams without changing reporting lines or roles, with the exception of Maya's shift to the senior leadership team. She emphasized how the culture of collaboration would unify staff, administrative teams, and partners around a shared purpose and create alignment across their diverse ministry Environments.

The boards of both ministries responded with cautious optimism. Some board members raised questions about how diagnostics would be used to identify inefficiencies and measure the effectiveness of MHOS. Greg and Emily responded with confident enthusiasm. They knew the power behind MHOS but recognized the need for clarity in the day-to-day application. Nonetheless, both shared their confidence that MHOS would establish a more unified approach to their ministries' missions.

## Engaging Senior Leadership Teams

After securing board approval, Greg and Emily moved on to engage their senior leadership teams, each inviting their communications directors—John for HRCC and Maya for FaithLink—to sit at the executive table for the first time.

At HRCC, Greg opened by explaining John's new role on the leadership team. "As we move forward with MHOS, communication is not just a support function; it's central to aligning our entire ministry with our mission. John's role here is essential because he brings the expertise and perspective to guide us in this alignment." Greg shared that MHOS wasn't about creating control but empowering every department to work toward a unified mission-driven approach. The team's reactions ranged from curiosity to hesitation, with some members questioning how this shift might impact their usual processes. Greg encouraged them to view MHOS as a way to reinforce, rather than disrupt, their goals, noting that John would be a strategic advocate in guiding the transition.

As Greg sensed the momentum building within the senior leadership team, he knew it was the perfect moment to unveil another pivotal shift. Taking a confident yet thoughtful tone, he began, "After some incredible conversations with Michael about the role of Executive Pastor (XP), we've decided together to redefine his title and focus. Moving forward, Michael will step into the role of Chief Culture Officer for Harvest Ridge, and the role of XP will be abandoned."

Greg paused, allowing the weight of the announcement to settle before continuing. "This shift isn't just about a title change—it's about aligning our leadership structure with what we've learned during the MHOS workshops. When I shared the formula for high-functioning dysfunction and the concept of sacred-cow tipping with Michael, he said something that resonated with me. He admitted that his greatest frustration with EOS has been how its focus on structure and metrics inadvertently fostered a culture of high-functioning dysfunction here at HRCC. I agreed with him that while it was worth trying, it was not a system that was serving us well as a church community. For the time being, we are pausing our emphasis on Rocks and quantitative metrics while we make these initial operational adjustments."

Greg's tone grew more hopeful. "Michael is ready to lead the charge in breaking down those silos and helping us cultivate a healthier, more mission-aligned ministry. This role will allow him to focus on the relational and cultural heartbeat of our church—ensuring that every department, every leader, and every decision reflects the mission we're called to fulfill. Michael and John will work closely with me to teach MissionHive to every staff member and volunteer leader, and to advocate for its principles and values in ways we believe will help us live out our calling more effectively."

Over at *FaithLink*, Emily addressed her leadership team with a similar introduction, welcoming Maya into her elevated role. She explained that Maya's addition to the senior leadership team would serve as a critical connection between FaithLink's mission and MissionHive's strategic framework. "With MHOS, communications isn't peripheral; it's the backbone of how we unify our message across all contexts. Maya's role here is to ensure that alignment, to keep us focused on our core purpose." Some leaders raised concerns about how Maya's strategic influence might alter the current dynamics, especially across global partnerships. Emily reassured them that Maya's expertise would be instrumental in fostering a cohesive narrative for FaithLink, especially within their unique field dynamics. No one was losing authority or responsibility, but everyone should be open to changes in their role if it meant making things work better.

As each of their teams processed these shifts, Greg and Emily invited them to "stack hands" on their commitment to bring MHOS to life within their ministries. They acknowledged that this journey would require trust, patience, and a shared commitment to the mission, especially as they each continued learning MHOS's nuances. Recognizing the challenges ahead, Greg and Emily encouraged their teams to view MHOS as a foundation for collaboration, one that would ultimately deepen their impact and strengthen every ministry area.

With this unified commitment, both HRCC and FaithLink prepared to embark on the journey of implementing MHOS, understanding that this would involve significant adjustments to their operational mindset. However, they were about to uncover a new area of tension: aligning their existing focus on quantitative goals with MHOS's mission-driven qualitative assessments.

## Exploring the Tensions of Measurement

As preparations progressed nicely week after week at Harvest Ridge and FaithLink, the shift toward MHOS began to surface questions about the role of measurement. For years, both ministries had relied on mostly quantitative metrics, KPIs and various lead-lag measures to assess certain aspects of success. Tracking attendance numbers, volunteers serving, and social media engagement had provided tangible insights—but not without challenges and limitations. As Greg and Emily adopted the MHOS approach with their teams, it became clear that both ministries would need to balance their quantitative insights with a fresh emphasis on qualitative measures to capture the true effect of their mission.

At HRCC, Pastor Greg's senior team, accustomed to the numbers focus of EOS, expressed a mix of anticipation and uncertainty. Such data, while concrete, had often pushed and pulled the church in ways that didn't always align with its true mission. Attendance counts, for example, didn't inherently reflect the quality of discipleship happening within the church. As Greg explained MHOS's focus on relational depth, spiritual growth, and community engagement, his leadership team realized they would need to redefine success in more holistic terms.

The team's reflection deepened as Michael shared insights from the MHOS workshops. "Numbers can be useful for certain benchmarks, but they often miss the core of what we're trying to accomplish in ministry," he noted. "With MHOS, we're being called to go beyond attendance metrics or volunteer counts to ask: Are people genuinely growing in their faith? Are they becoming increasingly involved in our thriving community because they are maturing? Are we with them each step of the way as they move toward relational involvement or advocacy?"

Greg affirmed Michael's point, acknowledging the complexity of the shift. "We're not eliminating quantitative data, but we're putting it in its rightful place where it is still relevant. I know this approach is new, and there will be times when it feels abstract for a while. But if we want to truly measure success, it has to be about more than numbers alone."

*At FaithLink*, Emily's senior team faced similar discussions. FaithLink's numerical goals had often centered on donor engagement—metrics that reassured supporters of the ministry's global reach and tangible achievements, alongside tracking donation income. However, as Maya and her communications team began considering how MissionHive's relational metrics could reshape donor relations, they found themselves balancing two priorities: providing numbers that demonstrated effectiveness and sharing the impactful stories that resonated with donors on a heart level.

A donor relations staff member voiced a common concern: "Will shifting focus to stories instead of numbers affect how our donors perceive our impact?"

David shared insights from the workshops, explaining that stories of lives transformed had a unique power to convey mission impact. "Numbers provide some sense of stability," he said, "but stories bring heart to the mission. When donors see the real outcomes of their support, they feel more connected to the mission."

Emily reinforced the importance of this balance, encouraging the team to see qualitative metrics as a way to enhance donor engagement rather than detract from it. "Our work is about transformation," she emphasized. "The more we bring our supporters into that story, the more aligned they become with our mission. Relationships drive mission, and advocacy from invested supporters could accomplish what no staff could do alone."

Emily continued, "And the beauty of that is, when we're measuring relationships instead of just numbers, we're giving ourselves permission to truly focus on people. We're building something much bigger than our own efforts. Sure, donations are essential to sustaining our work. However, we steward more than money–time, people, talent, energy–these all matter just as much."

As both HRCC and FaithLink grappled with these early tensions of measurement, Greg and Emily each recognized that aligning metrics with MHOS was about more than shifting data points; it was an opportunity to guide their teams toward a broader understanding of success. Preparing for Matt and Shawn's imminent return, they both knew the discussions on numerical versus relational metrics would only deepen. They hoped that MissionHive's founders would reveal helpful insights to authentically measure and celebrate the impact of their mission. First, though, they needed to continue addressing MHOS topics with their leadership teams.

## Steering Through the Complexity of Strategic Alignment

Both Greg and Emily found themselves wrestling with MHOS planning and strategic alignment within their organizations. Each senior leadership team, now informed about the core elements of MHOS, was eager to proceed, but some apprehensions remained.

## AT HRCC

Greg's primary challenge was maintaining the focus on MHOS while shifting the team's mindset away from merely executing tasks and toward aligning strategy with the mission. During one of the initial planning sessions, he noticed the tendency for team members to drift back into rushing to task lists and discussions centered on operational metrics, such as event attendance and volunteer count, which had long served as measures of success.

Greg regularly invited the team to reflect on the bigger picture. "These numbers can be useful, but are we measuring discipleship and spiritual growth, or just our capacity to attract people?" His question brought a reflective silence. "We now have Archetypes like Disciple, Seeker, and Parent. Let's think about what real engagement looks like for each one. What kind of metric, for instance, would signify that we're actually reaching Seekers and supporting them in their journey of faith exploration?"

John, newly on the senior leadership team, chimed in. "Right, it's not that we're ignoring numbers, but MHOS gives us the freedom to look beyond them—to see if we're truly moving people closer to faith or deeper into relationships."

Greg nodded. "Exactly. Instead of measuring just attendance or event participation, let's think about how we'd want a Parent or Volunteer Archetype to experience the church. Those relational dynamics are what MHOS is trying to get us to focus on."

He paused, reading a quote from his notebook that Shawn and Matt had shared earlier in the workshop: *"The most useful answers are the ones we take time to figure out ourselves—not the ones that everyone can find in a handbook."* Smiling, he added, "Maybe that's the heart of our work here—to figure out these answers in a way that's uniquely HRCC."

The leadership team engaged more deeply, recognizing that MHOS required them to dig into the relational aspects behind each Archetype, building an understanding that was specific to their congregation rather than relying on standard benchmarks.

## AT FAITHLINK

Emily and her leadership team at FaithLink were working through similar tensions, though with a different focus. Traditionally, their strategies relied heavily on tracking fieldwork impact and donor acquisition as primary indicators of success. However, with MHOS, Emily guided her team toward metrics that reflected the full mission of FaithLink.

"It's not about the number of donors we acquire but about the quality of relationships we build," she reminded the group. "Think about the journey of each of our Archetypes. With MHOS, we're creating pathways that invite them to journey with us toward advocacy, not just transaction."

Maya reminded the team, "We're here to build trust at every stage of the relationship—awareness, involvement, and ultimately, advocacy. MHOS is showing us that as we foster this journey with each donor, they're not only contributing financially but are becoming advocates who will encourage others to join. That's where we'll see the true impact."

As FaithLink's senior team redefined "impact," it began to reflect a commitment to relational depth. They saw that tracking how a donor progressed through each stage of their journey could be a powerful indicator of lasting success.

Emily sensed the weight of responsibility and a renewed excitement. "It's an adjustment, but if we keep our eyes on the mission and stay aligned with MHOS, we're setting ourselves up for connections that last beyond any one campaign or event. I want you to begin by focusing on how we can engage our General and Major Donors beyond just donating. How can we serve them and bring them so much delight in our relationship that they want to advocate for FaithLink Ministries among their friends and family?"

## Aligning Toward a Shared Vision

As both teams embraced the exploration of relational metrics, new questions occasionally emerged, but a deeper sense of purpose was taking root. The alignment that MHOS was fostering was reshaping their perspective, allowing each leader to see beyond the immediate tasks and numbers to the ultimate purpose—fulfilling their ministry's mission.

Both teams felt a mix of accomplishment and anticipation. Greg, Emily, and their leadership teams were more united than ever in their vision for aligning HRCC and FaithLink with the mission-first principles of MHOS. Yet, they knew this early adoption was only the beginning.

Greg took a moment with his team, expressing the value of these new conversations. "We're starting to see that success in ministry is less about reaching quotas and more about building genuine connections, fostering real discipleship, and helping people grow spiritually. But how do we measure that? Well, we've still got work to do." The team nodded, agreeing with his insight.

Over at FaithLink, Emily shared a similar sentiment. "We're developing a new vision for qualitative metrics that reflect our mission, but we're still finding our footing. And that's okay. The stories we tell and the lives we impact—those are our true measures of success. The challenge now is creating a framework that honors that. If we can keep progressing into this mindset, I think we're on the right path."

As each team prepared for this next phase in the process, they knew the journey ahead would be a rewarding one. The full implementation of MissionHive was on the horizon. Matt and Shawn's return was scheduled, and with it would come an exploration of measurements—moving beyond numbers and shaping metrics that tell the story of transformation at every level. Excitement was building, but there was still more to learn.

### Aha Moment

Greg and Emily began to see that measuring success through MHOS requires more than just tracking numbers—it involves redefining what success really means in ministry. By shifting their thinking toward qualitative, relational metrics, they saw the potential to move beyond transactional measures and toward capturing the depth of discipleship, community impact, and long-term engagement. The shift from traditional metrics to mission-aligned measures could provide a new perspective: success is not just what's counted but what's transformed.

### Reflect & Apply

Think about the metrics your ministry uses to define success. Are they primarily transactional, or do they reflect the deeper relational and spiritual growth aligned with your mission? Take a moment to identify one key area where you could integrate qualitative measures, such as stories of transformation or relational progress. How can these new metrics help your team see beyond the numbers and into the heart of the mission?

# CHAPTER FIFTEEN

# Moving from Numbers to Narratives

*"Not everything that can be counted counts, and not everything that counts can be counted."*

**William Bruce Cameron**

As the HRCC and FaithLink senior teams gathered once again in the familiar meeting room, there was an air of anticipation among all the participants. The weeks that passed since the initial workshops had given the two organizations a taste of what the MissionHive Operating System would require in each ministry context. Now, they were ready to share some of their insights with Matt, Shawn, and each other's leadership teams.

After some casual conversations and recapping the early days of implementation, Shawn opened up the floor for dialogue about metrics. "What have you been running into or realizing about measuring success and failure in the MissionHive system?"

Emily spoke first, capturing a sentiment shared by many. "Going back to HQ, I knew there'd be some challenges. But the reality is, there's a strong pull toward immediate and familiar numbers– attendance, donations, program outputs. Letting go of that for a more qualitative approach is proving to be a challenge."

Jeremy nodded. "We're having the same struggle. There's comfort in tracking measurable results. It feels almost risky to move towards a model that isn't as straightforward as simple numbers."

Shawn acknowledged the tension, his expression encouraging. "That's completely understandable. Shifting to a qualitative, narrative-based approach requires a different kind of trust. But it's also an invitation to recalibrate your definition of success so it aligns with your mission more deeply."

Matt chimed in with a grin, "To clarify, we're not saying to toss out quantitative metrics altogether. Teams like Finance, Accounting, and Donor Relations still need their data—the audits would be relentless!" The room erupted in laughter, lightening the discussion that felt intense from the outset.

"But seriously, even those metrics-driven teams need to stay mission-focused," Matt added. "I once worked with a church whose Executive Director of Operations, overseeing finance, facilities, and safety teams, got this. He had desk magnets made for his entire team that said, *'We make it easy for ministry to happen.'* That simple phrase was a daily reminder that even amidst essential logistics and numbers, they were serving the mission. Now *that's* a staff culture aligned with purpose!"

Maya Gonzalez shifted the conversation. "For us, the challenge isn't using stories of life change—it's leading with them. Donors still want to see those stories supplemented with clarity on financial needs, and later, with follow-up stories showing how the funds were used. It's finding that balance that I think will take time, and honestly some education along the way."

Emily nodded, adding, "Exactly. We're not trying to move away from accountability but to focus on the depth of transformation. This shift helps us bring the heart of our mission to the forefront without losing our transparency. It's a different view of stewardship."

Shawn smiled and started making a headlock gesture. "A former colleague of mine used to say that if you squeeze the numbers hard enough, they'll confess to anything." The room again erupted in laughter. Shawn continued, "This, of course, means that if we set all our goals on quotas and quantities, we risk losing sight of our mission. Even more seriously, we risk pushing God out of our ministry. Our mission is, well, our mission. Our messaging needs to reflect God's calling first and anything else is secondary."

Greg, visibly struck by Shawn's words, looked around the room. "Maybe we've relied on numbers to carry our message for too long. Our data shows growth, but it doesn't always show the depth of transformation. And while I know HRCC is impacting lives, if we're only tracking numbers and not this deeper engagement, we're missing the essence of our mission." He added, "though our attendance is high, our giving is not. In fact, because we haven't focused on spiritual transformation, we created a significant challenge for ourselves."

Emily echoed Greg's thoughts. "I feel the same. I want FaithLink to be known for the type of life change that reflects a deep commitment to our purpose."

Shawn smiled, recognizing the readiness in Greg and Emily's eyes. "That's why MHOS isn't about abandoning numbers altogether—it's about pairing them with stories of life change that truly capture the heartbeat of your mission. Numbers provide context and a kind of structure, but it's the stories that connect and inspire. Think of it this way: we're not saying numbers don't matter. We're simply suggesting a shift—leading with the stories that resonate deeply, and letting the numbers support those narratives. When you start with the transformation, the numbers naturally find their place. If you tell me 20 people were baptized last weekend, that is still encouraging. But if you tell me 20 stories about the people who were baptized, I'm engaged in a completely different way."

Matt moved the discussion forward, "Today, we'll explore this transition together, discussing examples of how both narratives and numbers can coexist effectively. This is about learning to spot what's already happening in your ministries that reflects these qualitative narratives."

## Biblical, Mission-Driven Metrics

As the session continued, Matt and Shawn guided the group into a deeper reflection on MHOS's mission-aligned metrics, highlighting how a truly ministry-focused approach could help both HRCC and FaithLink.

"To illustrate," Shawn said, "let's consider a story from 2 Samuel 24, when King David ordered a census. This wasn't just about counting people—it was an attempt to measure Israel's strength in numbers, placing security in human resources rather than God's provision. The impact was devastating. Seventy thousand people lost their lives because David put his strength in numbers instead of God."

The weight of that truth settled over the room. Emily broke the silence. "So, we're not just talking about adding a new layer to our metrics. We're talking about making sure our measurements align with our faith."

Matt nodded. "That's right, Emily. At HRCC and FaithLink, we're not in the business of building our own kingdoms. We're here to deepen relationships, lead people closer to God, and bear witness to transformation. Put another way, we exist to build God's Kingdom.

Your main focus should be on the life-changing journeys the numbers represent."

Shawn continued, "and that's where narrative metrics come into play. For example, in 1 Corinthians 3:7, Paul reminds us that *'neither he who plants nor he who waters is anything, but only God who gives the growth'* (Crossway, 2018). Our role is obedience and trust. Or think about Acts 2:41, where it says, 'those who received his word were baptized, and there were added that day about three thousand souls.' God gives growth, but He also shows us results tied to discipleship and obedience. Baptisms, discipleship engagement—those numbers have meaning because they are rooted in transformation."

Jeremy felt renewed. "It's a reminder that God multiplies our faithfulness, not necessarily our outputs. When we look at measurement this way, giving becomes about more than just contributions; it's about disciples on mission who give from a place of worship and obedience."

Matt agreed, noting, "Absolutely. The journey we invite people into is about transformation. MHOS lets us shift from simply measuring attendance or participation to measuring how well we're helping each Archetype progress in their relationship with God and His community."

Shawn added, "It's also about remembering that metrics don't define growth—God does. Jesus said in John 14:13, *'Whatever you ask in my name, this I will do, that the Father may be glorified in the Son'* (Crossway, 2018). Our calling isn't simply to produce results but to pray and trust God for the type of growth He wants to bring."

Matt jumped in, sharing a story to drive the point home. "A few years ago, I was part of a church capital campaign aiming to raise $1 million in three months. By the end of the campaign, they'd raised about $700,000. Now, here's where it got interesting: half the staff saw this as a failure because the goal wasn't fully met. But the other half celebrated what God had already provided and trusted Him to handle the rest—whether that meant additional funds or unexpected blessings in other ways."

He paused, letting the weight of the story settle in. "When you fixate solely on the metrics, you risk missing the bigger picture of how God is moving. The numbers are tools, not the whole story. Trusting God means leaving room for Him to work in ways you didn't anticipate, ways that may never show up on a spreadsheet or dashboard.

Emily nodded, understanding the vision. "So we need to look at metrics as a means to guide us, not to confine us. A ministry that captures people's stories, that's laser-focused on relational and spiritual transformation, will see numbers that matter—not just in scale, but in depth."

## Exploring Story-Driven Feedback Loops

Matt used Emily's insights as the opportunity to introduce the concept of "story-driven feedback loops"—a way to capture how real-life stories of ministry and impact could serve as indicators of mission alignment and success.

"What if we shifted our focus to listen for the stories that emerge from our daily ministry efforts?" he suggested. "Stories can reveal not only outcomes but also the journey—the context, the connections, the unexpected impacts—that numbers alone might miss."

Shawn expanded on this idea. "Think about the moments in your ministry that define why you're here. These aren't necessarily the big events or gatherings but are often small moments: a volunteer who finds their calling, a new disciple who takes their first steps of faith, or a family restored through a support group. Imagine each of those as a touchpoint." He paused then continued, "A lot of ministries go searching for the *best stories*—you know the ones. The dramatic transformations, the big, cinematic moments. And yes, those are powerful, but in chasing those, we often overlook the everyday victories—the smaller, more relatable stories that resonate just as deeply with people because they see themselves in them. The simple stories of some fishermen who left their boats to follow a Rabbi changed the course of history."

Emily looked thoughtful. "We've always shared stories in our reports, but we've seen them as separate from measurement— more like anecdotes."

"That's a common practice," Shawn agreed. "But in MHOS, stories aren't just supplemental—they're central. They become indicators of whether you're achieving your mission. Think of each story as a qualitative data point, something that offers evidence of transformation."

John spoke up, a light in his eyes. "So, instead of setting rigid goals, we're tuning into feedback that makes us ask, 'Is this truly working?' Are we meeting the needs of those we serve, and is our mission being fulfilled in the way we envisioned?"

Matt nodded. "Exactly. And when you view it that way, you're aligning each goal, each action, with your mission. As a team, you're not working toward arbitrary targets but actively ministering to your Archetypes—the reason your organization exists."

Shawn offered another example. "Have you ever offered a class that started with high attendance but then waned to the point almost no one showed up?" Heads nodded around the room. "Is that a reflection that the class served its purpose? Or that it's failing because no one is showing up? Your answers to those two questions will put you on a path to get more clarity. Maybe there isn't a problem. Or maybe the problem is simply the day and time the class is offered. This is how a story-driven feedback loop can use quantitative metrics to inform your analysis, but the 'why' of that metric is focused on the people the class is intended for."

The conversation naturally moved into practical ideas for integrating these story-driven metrics. Maya suggested gathering stories through regular feedback loops from volunteers, community partners, and even attendees at their outreach events. "We could ask them for specific examples of how the ministry has impacted their lives," she said. "Not only does that give us insight, but it also creates a culture of continuous feedback and improvement. We need to make sure we do it in a personal way."

Maya added, "And when we're listening to our Archetypes, we'll be tuned into what matters to them—beyond the data we capture. We'll be hearing what's truly reaching them, even if it's something unexpected. Our mission, then, becomes about guiding them through that entire relational journey."

Greg offered a final reflection on this topic. "We've measured so much by what's easy to count. But the truest metrics—the moments where lives intersect with God's grace—are the ones we can't always quantify. And yet, those are the ones that should define us."

Matt smiled and shared, "That's what we call *Kingdom Metrics*."

## Closing Insights and Preparing for the Shift

Matt and Shawn turned the focus back to each team, inviting them to share their reflections and thoughts on the transition they were about to make regarding measurement.

"Looking at your ministries now," Matt began, "how does it feel to be moving from a numbers-centered approach to one that emphasizes stories of life change? What challenges or opportunities do you still see?"

Greg, after a reflective pause, spoke first. "I can see how powerful this shift will be for us. Moving away from simply counting people or tracking activity allows us to look deeper at the discipleship journey. But honestly, I think it's going to feel unfamiliar—maybe even uncomfortable for some. Today helped me a lot, though."

Shawn nodded. "That's entirely normal, Greg. Metrics give us a sense of control, while stories—well, they're less predictable, less linear. But they offer a much richer understanding of what God is doing. And that's the heart of what ministries do: capture the relational and transformational aspects that can't always be captured by traditional metrics."

Emily added thoughtfully, "For FaithLink, I think it's going to be a big shift, especially for our donors and board. They've always been given detailed reports with numbers because it feels concrete, measurable. Now, we'll need to help them understand why stories can be just as powerful, if not more so, in showing impact."

Maya, sharing in the moment, suggested, "We could start by collecting specific stories from each of our Archetypes. Maybe it's a story of a donor moved by a report from the field, or a story of a staff member seeing the long-term impact of their work. It gives us concrete examples that are still rooted in personal transformation."

John, nodding, added, "This could be a way to highlight the diversity of experiences we see across our Archetypes' journeys. Each story is unique, but they all intersect with our mission. By showing how lives change, we're offering a picture of mission success that numbers alone can't capture."

Shawn offered a final piece of wisdom. "Remember, this shift doesn't happen overnight. MHOS isn't asking you to abandon everything you've ever done up to this point. It's inviting you to integrate—

bringing the numbers and stories together in a way that honors both your mission and the relationships that fuel it."

The room was filled with a renewed sense of purpose and direction, an awareness that this next stage would require patience, trust, and an openness to the unknown.

With that, the session concluded, leaving both teams with a sense of anticipation for the path ahead. They understood now that their new mission-driven metrics wouldn't simply reflect performance; they'd become a testament to the Kingdom impact of their ministries.

### Aha Moment

As both HRCC and FaithLink teams embraced the shift from quantitative to qualitative assessment, they recognized that success in ministry isn't defined by numbers alone, but by stories that reflect true life transformation. This new perspective invited them to focus on discipleship, relational impact, and spiritual growth—offering a fuller, mission-centered understanding of success.

### Reflect & Apply

Consider the current metrics in your ministry or organization. What might you be missing if you only look at quantitative data? Reflect on one or two stories that illustrate your mission in action. How could these stories help your team better understand and communicate the impact of your work?

# CHAPTER SIXTEEN

# Preparing to Launch MHOS

*"You don't have to see the whole staircase,
just take the first step."*

**Martin Luther King Jr.**

**A**s the senior leadership teams of HRCC and FaithLink finalized plans to introduce the MissionHive Operating System across their entire organizations, both Greg and Emily recognized the careful planning needed to ensure MHOS's success. This launch marked a pivotal moment, not only for their ministries but for each of their teams as they transitioned into a system that prioritized mission, relational Environments, and dynamic collaboration. The rollout would be gradual, intentionally designed to align with each ministry's unique needs and cultures while maintaining a consistent focus on MHOS's principles.

## Defining Structure and Mission Alignment

The first step was establishing a new structure for daily and weekly operations across both ministries. Each team designed meeting agendas around the MHOS pillars and key concepts, beginning with regular mission-centered discussions that aligned with the specific Environments and Archetypes each ministry served. These meetings would reinforce each team's understanding of their mission-focused role, fostering alignment and shared ownership at every level of the organization.

In preparation for this shift, Greg and Emily planned to introduce MHOS in well-paced stages. New senior leadership meeting structures—inspired by the MHOS Hive Effect, diagnostics, and story-driven feedback models—ensured two-directional communication while enabling real-time feedback from across HRCC's campuses and FaithLink's regional networks. This alignment helped both organizations stay focused on the relational impact of their work, empowering them to address potential gaps or silos in real time.

## Training Staff and Creating a Culture of Adaptive Learning

Next, Greg and Emily set priorities for introducing all staff to MHOS and the beecosystem. In training sessions led by their senior teams, they focused on practical applications of MHOS while fostering a culture of adaptive learning. Staff were encouraged to think critically and collaboratively, viewing their work through the lens of the Archetypes they served and aligning their goals with broader ministry Environments.

Greg and Emily emphasized that MHOS was not merely an operating system but a philosophy empowering staff to prioritize mission-aligned goals. A central component was granting staff the ability to say "no" to initiatives that fell outside the mission scope, thus preventing scope creep. While this was difficult for some at first, this autonomy fostered ownership and collaboration, encouraging each team member to actively engage with MHOS principles while refining them in practice.

With an adaptive learning culture, staff moved beyond simple task fulfillment to become active contributors to the broader mission. Every staff member was given a clear role in this system, provided with the tools to balance strategic goals with day-to-day operations, empowered to adapt and align messages and activities to best function in their ministry Environments.

## Establishing Metrics and Feedback Loops

In tandem with staff training, Greg and Emily recognized the need to clarify how MHOS would reshape their approach to measurement. Rather than relying solely on quantitative metrics, they focused on qualitative indicators that aligned with MHOS's mission-first philosophy, capturing elements of relational and spiritual transformation. While numeric data points remained valuable, especially for Finance, Donor Relations, Facilities and Accounting teams, HRCC and FaithLink would now prioritize qualitative stories of life change, as well as engagement levels across each of their unique Environments.

Both ministries also incorporated feedback loops into their meeting rhythms, allowing staff to share insights on what was working and where adjustments were needed. These loops served as real-time diagnostics, enabling the leadership teams to make course corrections as necessary, maintaining focus on relational and spiritual outcomes. The emphasis on qualitative assessment re-centered both organizations around life-change that demonstrated mission impact beyond traditional metrics, ensuring that staff at all levels could contribute to a holistic understanding of success.

## Fostering Engagement

Finally, as the launch was well under way, Greg and Emily knew that sustaining MHOS would require an intentional blend of clarity and encouragement. By positioning MHOS as a framework that brought focus to both the "how" and "why" of their work, they emphasized that this shift wasn't merely operational but was designed to deepen alignment with each ministry's purpose.

Both leaders highlighted the importance of every staff member's voice and feedback in the process, inviting a commitment to "stack hands" and move forward together. They reminded their teams that, although the initial stages of MHOS implementation would require adjustments and continuous learning, this unified approach would ultimately empower them to serve their Archetypes with greater depth and purpose.

With preparations complete, Greg and Emily felt assured that their teams were equipped to embrace this new chapter. They, along with their senior leadership teams, were prepared to provide ongoing support and guidance. Recognizing that these organizational changes might spark shifts in staffing needs or roles, HR was also at the ready.

The launch of MHOS symbolized more than the adoption of a new system—it was a renewed pledge to a mission-first, relationally driven philosophy poised to redefine how HRCC and FaithLink connected with and served their communities.

## Aha Moment

As they prepared for the shift to the MissionHive Operating System, the leadership teams at both organizations realized the importance of not just adopting a new system but embodying it in their own interactions. They came to understand that successful implementation begins with leaders modeling MHOS principles in tangible ways—communicating openly, listening actively, and supporting each other across departments.

## Reflect & Apply

Consider your own leadership or team culture. What practical steps could you take to embody the mission and values of your organization more visibly? Write down two or three specific ways you can model transparency, collaboration, and support within your context to pave the way for cultural transformation.

# Part 7: Long-Term Success and Sustainability

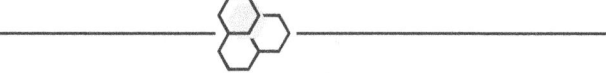

## Hive Insight

In this penultimate part, readers gain insight into the sustainability and long-term impact of the MissionHive Operating System by reflecting on its adoption within HRCC and FaithLink one year after implementation began. Through the experiences of these two organizations, readers see MHOS's enduring effect and learn how to maintain its effectiveness amidst growth and change.

# CHAPTER SEVENTEEN

# Lasting Impact and First Year Reflections

*"And let us not grow weary of doing good, for in due season we will reap, if we do not give up."*

**Galatians 6:9**

**G**reg Johnson reclined comfortably in his chair at HRCC, exchanging a reflective look with Matt. "A year in, MissionHive has become a lot more than a set of processes. It's changed how we think about everything we do here. We're no longer trying to manage all these scattered priorities. We're moving with one focus, one mission."

Matt nodded, noting Greg's shift in confidence. "I remember when we started, you wondered if this would mean letting go of too much. How do you feel about those sacred cows now?"

Greg chuckled. "I have to admit, there were some cows I thought we'd never tip over. Take our Easter carnival. Every year we'd bring in a petting zoo, bounce houses, you name it. It was a huge draw. It was no doubt more an entertainment event than anything mission-driven. With MHOS in place, we took a step back and asked ourselves if it aligned with the purpose. So we replaced it with 'Community Connections Day.' Instead of entertainment, we offered spaces for families to meet with small group leaders and find ways to engage with HRCC. It was a risk, but in the end, we had more people signing up for groups and volunteer roles than we ever did with the carnival. And not stopping there, the health of our groups has increased along with the quantity. I'm seeing real community forming in the groups, a vision I've had for over 20 years. We wrongly believed that if we didn't lead with fun, no one would come. People can find fun everywhere today. It's deep community connection that eludes so many."

Across town at FaithLink, Emily Roberts shared a similar reflection with Shawn. "It wasn't easy letting go of some of our long-held traditions.

For instance, our 'Legacy Celebration Dinner'—that was a true sacred cow. It had always been about honoring our top donors, complete with an elaborate slideshow of anything donors supported in the last year. Half the night was dedicated to that slideshow, and you could just see people checking out."

Shawn raised an eyebrow. "How did MHOS help you address that?"

"We refocused the evening on stories from the field. Instead of just recognizing donors, we created mixed tables where they sat with volunteers and staff. They heard firsthand how their support made an impact while getting to know others relationally. It was personal, and by the end of the night, we'd not only raised more funds than ever before but had deeper conversations. MHOS gave us permission to move past routine and create something that really mattered."

## Core Principles Emerging from MHOS

As Matt and Shawn continued to meet with Greg and Emily, they found that their year-long MHOS journey had revealed several lasting principles that went beyond operations, transforming each organization's culture and focus.

## Mission-Centered Decision-Making

Greg looked back on the changes MHOS had helped HRCC implement. "The Hive Effect was a game-changer. Before MHOS, we used to jump on board with almost any community event as long as it drew a crowd. Now, we filter everything through the mission. One example was our partnership with the city for the annual Christmas tree lighting. For the city, it's about entertainment, but we refocused it as 'Family on Mission.' We brought in small group leaders and ministry partners to meet with families, creating real connections. Our participation in church activities afterward skyrocketed."

At FaithLink, Emily reflected, "For us, MHOS helped us examine programs that had been part of FaithLink for years. We had 'Open Tables' gatherings designed to bring people together over a shared meal, but over time, it had lost its purpose. It was more social than anything, and the original heart behind it—connecting newcomers to FaithLink's mission—had been forgotten. We were essentially preaching our message to ourselves because no one new attended anymore. We transformed 'Open Tables' into 'Community Circles,' a pretty subtle name change that allowed us the opportunity to reset. Now, every meal centers around a structured time for conversation and attendees have to bring a friend. When Mary registers, she registers for two and has to then invite someone. We found it kind of gamifies the event and offers our attendees a natural way to invite their friends. At the event, field coordinators and volunteers share personal stories about the mission, but we also get to know the guests. The 'Community Circles' ended up bringing the original heart of 'Open Tables' back to life. Now, everyone who attends is either an Advocate or completely lacks any awareness of FaithLink. Both groups, and our team, love it because they feel part of something meaningful by the end."

Shawn nodded. "That's the beauty of mission-centered decision-making—it's about saying 'no' to what doesn't align so you can say a resounding 'yes' to what truly matters. I love the innovation with those Community Circles. You didn't reinvent the wheel, you made the event fit the Hive Effect. Genius!"

## Adaptability with Boundaries

HRCC and FaithLink both found that MHOS provided a flexible framework that didn't force them to choose between consistency and adaptability.

Greg described how Diagnostics became a "growth compass" at HRCC. "As we consider expanding to new campuses, Diagnostics have allowed us to identify areas where we're mission-aligned and areas where we need more focus. It's made growth feel intentional instead of transactional because we look at our surrounding communities and ask ourselves, 'Where is a church like HRCC most needed?' It brings purity to the process. Instead of adding locations just because we can, we're doing it in a way that supports the mission from the outset." He continued, "It's even led us to consider partnerships with other churches in certain areas, before just planting another HRCC campus. We're all on the same team, let's act like it!"

For Emily at FaithLink, adaptability meant learning to customize programs based on regional needs without losing mission alignment. "FaithLink is international, so we had to learn to adapt our strategies and actions within the missional focus. We used Diagnostics to let each region shape the execution of their programs in ways that make sense locally. One region even created its own volunteer training based on cultural needs. But because everything connects back to our core mission, we're not just adapting for the sake of it. We're adapting with purpose. And even with that custom volunteer training, HQ was involved from the beginning–not dictating but learning how we can improve."

## Empathy and Archetype Engagement

Both organizations found that MHOS's empathy-based approach brought new depth to their understanding of the people they serve.

Greg shared how "Serve and See" sessions became instrumental in connecting staff to HRCC's mission. "Every month, our staff members spend a day visiting with outreach volunteers and official community partners. Whether it's shadowing a volunteer group, attending a small group meeting, or stocking shelves at the food bank, these 'Serve and See' days help our staff understand firsthand how all our activities tie into the bigger picture. One of our newer team members said it was the first time he truly saw himself as part of the mission. It's not just a 'day out'–it's a way to build purpose and connection. Each department debriefs the day after and shares important observations or conversations that shape our future efforts."

For FaithLink, Emily introduced "Mission Mapping" sessions to show volunteers how their roles connect to the mission. "This idea came from Sarah Njoroge. You insisted we bring someone from a role like hers to the workshop and she just ran with the opportunity. She knew that our volunteers often felt like they were just filling a role. By mapping their journey and showing them potential pathways, she helped them see they're part of something bigger. It's been amazing to see some of those volunteers move into leadership roles because they finally feel like they have a place in the mission. They aren't helping us, they are us. We cannot exist without them, and we ensure they know we value them. We flew Sarah to train all our other regions. She is thriving in MissionHive."

## Reflections on Long-Term Resilience and Lasting Impact

As their conversations with Matt and Shawn continued, Greg and Emily shared broader reflections on MHOS's impact and the lasting resilience it had brought to their organizations.

## Sustaining Mission Alignment

Emily reflected with Shawn on how MHOS's feedback loops kept FaithLink aligned, even in challenging times. "We started quarterly check-ins to gather feedback from our teams. There was one check-in where some of our field coordinators said they felt disconnected. Using Diagnostics to uncover the issue, we created more frequent 'Regional Field Story' sessions where regional staff gather to share updates and field insights. For international teams, we host monthly virtual Field Story sessions, connecting our global network without the costs of in-person travel. It's a simple, sustainable adjustment that's made a huge difference in keeping everyone connected to our successes."

Greg shared with Matt that HRCC's feedback process had uncovered the need for more consistent support for small group leaders. "They were struggling to see their impact, so we created a network where they could share success stories and challenges. We started a weekly message that looped them into what we had coming up so they could Advocate connection opportunities with their group members. That simple step of serving them lifted them up and encouraged them that their work is vital. We needed the Archetype journeys to help us see we had stopped communicating with them once they started leading a group, so we corrected it."

## Building a Mission-Driven Culture

Greg and Emily both found that MHOS had moved beyond being a strategy to become an integral part of their organization's Identity. It was truly their beecosystem.

"It's been incredible to see MHOS turn into a culture," Greg highlighted. "We used to focus on events and attendance, but now we focus on engagement and impact. We have new onboarding processes for staff and volunteers that introduce them to our mission from day one. They don't just join HRCC—they become part of the mission. They are taught the Hive Effect and given the Archetype journeys and Environments." He continued, his eyes welling up with tears, "Watching Michael transition from the role of a traditional XP to embracing his new position as our Chief Culture Officer has been nothing short of incredible. He's not just thriving in this role—he's making an enormous impact on our team and our mission. Just the other day, he told me that stepping into this role reminded him why he left the world of technology for ministry in the first place. He is a unique gift to the Harvest Ridge community."

Emily modeled FaithLink's onboarding on Harvest Ridge's design. She shared with Shawn, "Greg's team got to onboarding before we did in our implementation. Two of my HR staff were on maternity leave, so I asked our HR director to meet with Greg's team. She was so impressed with what they created, she just boldly asked if we could copy them. She adapted some things for our context, certainly. The fact we could borrow from their MHOS ideas was such an added benefit I didn't initially think about. It's the beauty of the beecosystem—everyone can help anyone!"

## Closing Reflection

At HRCC, Greg shared his final thoughts with Matt. "For us, MHOS has been a collective movement, not just a framework. It's something that feels alive. It guides us forward, but it also keeps us grounded. We're not just running programs—we're serving the mission in a way that feels sustainable and purpose-driven."

At FaithLink, Emily reflected with Shawn on MHOS's overall impact. "It's given us clarity that's hard to describe. MHOS isn't just a strategy. It's a commitment to who we are, a reminder that everything we do must connect back to the mission. It's helped us create a culture that doesn't just chase growth or activity but seeks meaning in every action we take. We are such good stewards of what God has entrusted to us. And when I meet with major donors or other organizational executives, I boldly tell them how God is using us."

Both organizations experienced some staff turnover during the transition. For those who found that the changes didn't align with their strengths or passions, leadership worked intentionally to help them transition out of the organization and into new roles where they could thrive. This shift created opportunities to bring in new team members who were fully aligned with the mission, strengthening the overall culture and focus of the teams in a healthy way.

Matt and Shawn left HRCC and FaithLink, knowing that MissionHive had not only transformed two organizations—it had redefined what it meant for them to be mission-driven. For both organizations, the honey was flowing.

**Aha Moment**

As HRCC and FaithLink's leaders reflected on the past year, they realized that MHOS had done more than realign their programs—it had redefined how they approached every decision. By anchoring each action to the mission, MHOS had transformed their organizations into purpose-driven communities. They saw that this clarity empowered their teams to let go of traditions that had lost their meaning, making room for genuine, lasting engagement.

**Reflect & Apply**

As you read this chapter, did Emily or Greg's reports resonate with you? Do you sense familiar elements of your ministry's challenges in the HRCC or FaithLink stories? Make a list of things on which MissionHive could help your ministry refocus. Pray about these things, asking God to help you know what your next steps could be.

# Part 8: MissionHive OS and Your Ministry

# CHAPTER EIGHTEEN

# Exploring MHOS for Your Ministry

*"Uncharted territory does not make our experience, education, and expertise irrelevant, just incomplete."*

**Tod Bolsinger**

## Dear Sisters and Brothers,

You're reading this because something in your heart led you to ministry. Maybe you've felt that calling for as long as you can remember, or maybe it grew over time as you saw lives touched by God's grace. Either way, you know, as we do, that ministry is more than what we do—it's an expression of who we are. It's our way of reflecting God's love, offering hope, and building a community where every person can find their place in His story.

But we know the reality too. Ministry, rooted in love and calling, is full of real-life pressures and challenges. The day-to-day demands pull us in different directions, the programs and structures we build can feel like walls that keep us from reaching one another, and even the most genuine passion can be dimmed by the sheer weight of it all.

That's why we created *MissionHive OS*. We didn't set out to build just another system or introduce a list of tasks. Instead, we imagined a way to let the heartbeat of ministry shine through everything we do. We wanted something that could bring clarity before things become chaotic, that could unify our work without stifling it, and that could help each person, each role, find its true connection to the mission we share.

*MissionHive* isn't here to replace what makes your ministry unique; it exists to honor and elevate it. It's not a rigid plan or a set of rules. It's a framework that helps you stay connected to what really matters, so every step, every conversation, every act of service reflects the love and purpose that brought you to ministry in the first place.

*MissionHive OS* is our living love letter to the global Church, to all who minister every day around the world, whatever your environment or mission-focus, and to every individual shown the love of God because your ministry exists.

Our prayer is that *MissionHive* helps you rediscover the joy and purpose of your calling. May it bring your team closer together, remind you of the beauty in what you're building, and create a community where each person feels seen, valued, and connected to the mission.

If you're feeling like you now have as many questions as answers, take heart and remember the wisdom we shared earlier from Bernadette Jiwa: *"The most useful answers are the ones we take time to figure out ourselves—not the ones that everyone can find in a handbook."* True clarity often comes from the process of discovery, not from quick solutions. God's Spirit will guide you.

Thank you for all you do, and welcome to MissionHive OS. We're honored to walk this journey with you.

With faith, love, and encouragement,

**Shawn and Matt**

# 1. MissionHive Alignment Assessment

This assessment invites you to reflect on how well your ministry aligns with the principles of MissionHive OS. Organized around Mission-First Alignment, Relationship-Driven Communication Flow, Empowerment Over Control, and Positively-Charged Diagnostics, it provides a holistic lens to evaluate your ministry's current state and areas for growth.

## Reflection Prompts

### Mission-First Alignment: The Core Purpose

Anchoring all strategy and communication to the mission ensures every initiative advances your ministry's purpose.

1. Do your ministry's programs and activities consistently reflect and support your mission, or are there initiatives that have drifted from their purpose?
2. How often does your leadership team assess whether programs are mission-aligned? Is there a clear process for making those decisions?
3. Are your metrics—such as attendance, giving, or volunteer engagement—rooted in relational outcomes that reflect your mission?
4. How do you intentionally connect staff, volunteers, and stakeholders to your mission so they feel a deep sense of purpose in their roles?

### Relationship-Driven Communication Flow: Living the Hive Effect

The **Hive Effect** ensures dynamic, two-way communication that connects the mission (Identity) to the people you serve (Archetypes) through strategic Environments.

1. How are Archetypes included in your communication strategies? Are their unique journeys and needs reflected in how you engage with them?
2. Is communication in your ministry open and dynamic, or do silos or top-heavy structures limit collaboration and feedback?
3. Are you regularly sharing stories of transformation and impact, and are they used to inspire decisions and align messaging?

4. Do your strategic Environments—such as gatherings, small groups, or outreach—serve as spaces where mission, Archetypes, and communication intersect meaningfully?

## Empowerment Over Control: Building a Beecosystem

Thriving ministries empower team members at every level to contribute their unique gifts while remaining aligned with the mission.

1. Are team members trusted and empowered to make mission-aligned decisions in their areas of responsibility?
2. How does your ministry equip staff and volunteers to understand and embody the mission in their daily work?
3. Is creativity encouraged in your ministry, or does maintaining the status quo limit innovation?
4. Does every team member—whether staff or volunteer—understand their value within the broader mission?

## Positively-Charged Diagnostics: Fuel for Growth

MissionHive's diagnostics encourage ministries to uncover challenges and opportunities without fear of judgment, fostering a culture of learning and growth.

1. Do you regularly conduct debriefs or reflections after major events or programs to evaluate success and opportunities for improvement?
2. Are diagnostic tools used to uncover root causes of challenges, or do you rely on surface-level fixes?
3. How do you ensure that diagnostics are constructive rather than punitive, encouraging trust and openness among teams?
4. Are there "sacred cows" in your ministry—traditions or processes that have outlived their mission-aligned purpose? How are these addressed constructively?
5. Are diagnostic insights shared across teams to create a shared understanding and inform future strategies?

# 2. Exploring Your MissionHive Journey

If you recognize MHOS as a potential fit, begin with these exploratory steps. They offer manageable ways to test or introduce MHOS principles without full implementation, giving you a practical feel for how it can shape your ministry.

## Step 1: Revisit or Clarify the Mission

Take time to revisit your mission statement. Consider if it's central to your ministry's operations and effectively guides decisions and actions. Engage your team in refining the mission, if needed, to foster a shared understanding of purpose.

## Step 2: Evaluate Ministry Environments

Identify the Environments within your ministry and assess if each Environment reflects and supports the mission. Are these spaces inviting people to connect meaningfully with the mission, or could they be realigned for greater impact?

## Step 3: Identify and Engage Archetypes

Consider key Archetypes within your community and explore their motivations and needs. Archetype development often requires team input, but you can begin by using a sample Archetype (such as those from FaithLink or HRCC) to gain an initial understanding of empathy mapping in your context. Define touchpoints and ministry responses for the Archetype to see how MissionHive's empathy-driven approach can strengthen connections.

## Step 4: Try the Hive Effect

Select a decision or program and apply the Hive Effect, using your Archetype to evaluate mission alignment. Start by identifying the decision's intended impact on this group and assess how it flows through your organizational structure. Does it strengthen mission alignment, or does it introduce complexity without a clear purpose? Do you encounter resistance that reflects misalignment?

## Step 5: Experiment with Diagnostics Using the HfD Formula

Use the HfD formula to examine a successful program or area of ministry for underlying issues that might be impacting mission alignment. Focus on identifying signs of *High-Functioning Dysfunction* (HfD) by asking these questions:

- *Tactics before Strategy* (TbS): Are we focusing on tactical activities that keep us busy but lack a clear mission-centered strategy?

- *False Consensus Effect* (FCE): Are we assuming our team and the communities we serve understand, agree with, and feel connected to our mission, without verifying this?

- *Cycles of Responsiveness* (CoR): Are we caught in a reactive cycle, addressing immediate issues as they arise instead of proactively planning with the mission in mind?

If all three elements of HfD are present negatively, your organization may be experiencing hidden misalignments. Symptoms can include high turnover, siloed departments, dissatisfied Archetypes, reactive scrambling rather than proactive planning, frequent task-driven meetings with limited strategic outcomes, and mission scope creep. Apply these questions to one area of ministry to determine if surface-level success is masking deeper alignment needs. Lookout for sacred cows along the way.

# 3. Encouragement for the Journey

As you consider implementing MHOS, remember that it is a versatile, adaptable framework designed to support organizations with various operational structures. Whether your ministry already uses a system like EOS (as seen at HRCC) or operates without a formal framework but follows traditional organizational structure (as seen at FaithLink), MHOS offers a communications-centered beecosystem that places the mission at the heart of operations.

MHOS does not dictate formal structures, accountability lines, or HR policies. Instead, it creates an atmosphere in which communication plays a central role, encouraging leaders, volunteers, and community members to take active roles in collaborative decision-making and problem-solving. MHOS will guide you in creating alignment and cohesion, but leadership and strategic decision-making remain essential.

Embracing MHOS empowers ministries to renew and refocus, connecting purpose with action and creating a mission-driven culture that thrives on clarity, empathy, and strategic alignment. As you move forward, know that you are not only enhancing your organization but also joining a larger movement of purpose-driven ministries committed to mission-first impact.

Just as bees contribute to the health of ecosystems far beyond their hives, a mission-driven organization positively influences its surrounding community and networks. Through intentional collaboration, alignment with core values, and a clear focus on the mission, your church or nonprofit becomes more than just a collection of teams—it becomes a catalyst for transformation. Bees don't just serve their hives; their work sustains plant life, biodiversity, and agricultural productivity. In the same way, a unified, purpose-driven organization can extend its impact far beyond its own walls, creating lasting change in the lives of those it touches.

# REFERENCES

Brown, D. (2021, September 1). *Story Archetypes: How to Recognize the 7 Basic Plots - 2024*. MasterClass. Retrieved November 19, 2024, from https://www.masterclass.com/articles/a-guide-to-story-Archetypes

Crossway. (2018). *ESV Church Bible*. Crossway.

Eyal, N., & Li, J. (2019). *Indistractable: How to Control Your Attention and Choose Your Life*. BenBella Books.

Jiwa, B. (2014). *Marketing: A Love Story, How to Matter to Your Customers*. Story of Telling Press.

# LIST OF ILLUSTRATIONS

# ABOUT THE AUTHORS

**Shawn Boyd** is a seasoned leader with over 25 years of experience in marketing, communications, fundraising, and operations across business, global missions, and multi-campus church ministry. His work—shaped by engagement in more than 35 countries—offers a unique perspective on the cultural and operational challenges faced by churches and nonprofits.

He holds a BA in Communications from Moody Bible Institute and an MA in Executive Leadership from Liberty University's Graduate School of Business. Shawn specializes in integrating communication and operational systems to align entire organizations, strengthen front-line ministry, and advance both mission and spiritual transformation.

As co-author of MissionHive OS, Shawn helps organizations align ministry objectives with their core values and purpose, emphasizing relational engagement, operational clarity, and sustainable impact.

Shawn and his wife, Laura, have been married for over 25 years and are the proud parents of two daughters, Savannah and Brooklyn, and one son, Donovan. Together, they enjoy serving their church community, exploring global ministry opportunities, and spending time as a family.

**Matt Wish** is a creative leader with over a decade of experience guiding high-performing marketing, communications and creative teams across corporate, non-profit, and ministry spaces. His work is defined by a passion for storytelling and innovation.

Matt holds a BS in Communications from Grand Valley State University. As the founder and CEO of Sonder Marketing & Design, Matt specializes in turning complex ideas into actionable strategies centered on mission. Whether crafting compelling narratives through multiple mediums or designing innovative campaigns, his approach is rooted in the belief that strategy should always come before tactics.

From his start as a college intern to serving on a senior leadership team in Communications at a multi-site church, Matt brings a rich understanding of ministry dynamics to his work.

A seasoned leader, worship leader, YouTuber, writer, and creative visionary, Matt has honed a diverse skill set by following his passions. As co-author of MissionHive OS, Matt equips churches and nonprofits to move beyond self-promotion toward authentic, mission-centered engagement and self-disclosure.

Matt and his wife Bethany have been married for 15 years. They live in North Carolina with their two wild boys, Jack and Finn, where faith, creativity, and adventure shape their daily lives.

www.ingramcontent.com/pod-product-compliance
Lightning Source LLC
Chambersburg PA
CBHW061751120626
46550CB00005B/1954